The Lord's
MOUNT OLIVET
PROPHECY

The Lord's MOUNT OLIVET PROPHECY

John Allfree

BIBLE STUDY PUBLICATIONS
1 Penrith Place, Mansfield, Nottinghamshire NG19 6NE, UK

First Published 1996
Second Edition 2006

ISBN 0 9528509 1 5

Front cover: Relief from the Arch of Titus showing Jews being led into captivity with furniture from the Temple.

Bible Study Publications
1 Penrith Place • Mansfield • NG19 6NG • UK

Printed and bound by Printland Publishers
G.P.O. Box 159 • Hyderabad • 500 001 • India

Other works by the author:

A World Destroyed by Fire
An exposition of 2 Peter 3 showing from Scripture its application to the overthrow of Israel in AD 70 — A5 booklet, 34 pages.

Demon Possession and the Bible
A Biblical approach to an intriguing and sometimes perplexing subject — A5 booklet, 16 pages.

Edom in Bible Prophecy
Attempts to make sense of the end-time prophecies involving Edom and sets out to answer such questions as: Does 'Edom' simply represent the Gogian confederacy or a could it be a group of Arab nations? Will the Arabs overthrow Israel? — book, 93 + vii pages.

Ezekiel
A detailed exposition of chapters 1-39 of this major prophetic book — hardcover book, 472 pages. (Published by CSSS.)

Faith and Conversion
Examines the process of conversion and answers the question: What part is played by the holy spirit in the process? A much needed restatement of the Christadelphian view of this important subject — A5 booklet, 17 pages.

The Cherubim
Concentrates on the principles that lead to an understanding of the cherubim in Scripture — A5 booklet, 40 pages.

Trinitarian Texts Examined
Examines the Bible passages that are used by trinitarians to support the doctrine — A5 booklet, 50 pages.

ACKNOWLEDGEMENTS

The substance of this book first appeared, in embryo form, as a series of addresses given in the mid 1970s at the Stoke Rochford Bible School and in 1977 those talks were published in the *Bible Student* magazine. The arguments set out in those addresses and articles attracted considerable interest and no little criticism. I am grateful to those critics who made me think again and sent me back to "search the scriptures… whether those things were so."

The first edition of *The Lord's Mount Olivet Prophecy* followed in 1996 and whilst the earlier efforts had concentrated on Matthew ch. 24, in the book attention was also given to those differences that appear in the parallel records, especially in the Gospel of Luke. A number of fellow Bible students — among whom my son, Mark, deserves special mention — read the manuscript, or part of it, and offered helpful criticism and suggestions, which helped shape the finished work. I must now also thank those who, having read the first edition, contacted me with suggestions and encouragement that have been useful in the preparation of this new edition.

For permission to include photographs/pictures in this edition I thank:

- Prof. Todd Bolen, BiblePlaces.com* for the photographs on the front cover and on pages 6, 43 and 115.
- Alec Gerard and Ritmeyer Architectural Design for the picture of the Temple model by Alec Gerard on page 5.
- Bible Picture Gallery (*www.CC-Art.com*) for the illustrations on pages 54 and 60.
- George Eastman House Photographic Museum for the picture on page 94.

I am grateful to Chris Parkin for his invaluable help with proofreading and for his many editorial suggestions.

---

* I recommend a visit to *www.BiblePlaces.com* — request the Bible Places Newsletter which comes with free down-loadable coloured photographs and details of superb collections for purchase.

I again record my indebtedness to my wife, Maureen, for her patience, help, and encouragement in this and all other aspects of work in the Master's service.

Finally I express my thanks to "the Father of mercies and the God of all comfort" for blessing me with the health, time and opportunity to pursue my studies of His word.

J.A.

PREFACE

The subject of the Olivet Prophecy has occupied my mind for many years. In the mid 1960s a chance encounter with a series of articles, in the then out of print *Herald of the Kingdom and Age to Come,* entitled "The Last Days of Judah's Commonwealth", written by John Thomas, directed me to look at the Olivet Prophecy in a way that had not previously occurred to me. I have, in the intervening years, pursued the carefully reasoned arguments there set out in connection with the third chapter of Peter's second letter, to a logical conclusion with respect to the Olivet Prophecy.

The careful observer will have noted that all is not well in the way in which use is made of the Olivet Prophecy in Christadelphian teaching. One hears the "wars and rumours of wars" (Matt. 24:6) and the "famines, and pestilences, and earthquakes, in divers places" (Matt. 24:7) variously ascribed to modern conflicts and disasters by some, and to events in the apostolic period by others. The preaching of the gospel of the kingdom in all the world (Matt. 24:14) is assigned to modern missionary activities by some, but applied to first century preaching by others. There are those who maintain that the events foretold by Jesus have a full application both to the apostolic period and also to modern times. Others approach the Olivet Prophecy from what is often referred to as a 'continuous historical' standpoint. However, this is a misnomer for it seems to mean simply that they pick and choose what parts of the prophecy will be placed in the AD 70 period and what parts will be given 'a latter-day' application. Those who adopt this approach pick and choose differently. Recently the futurist approach, which sees the entire prophecy as having exclusive application to the end-time period leading up to the second advent, has resurfaced. Altogether a most unsatisfactory situation.

The confident prediction by many that "this generation" (Matt. 24:34, said to be about 40 years) that witnessed the re-establishment of the State of Israel in 1948 would see the return of Jesus, for many years seemed to me to be ill-founded and, with the passage of time, was shown to be so. This alone should have alerted all serious Bible students who subscribed to that view, to the need for a serious re-examination of the Olivet Prophecy.

The book is intentionally challenging. I have tried to be accurate and fair in quotations and in criticism of other writers. I ask only that others will afford me the same courtesy, as the exposition set out in these pages is subjected to welcome critical evaluation.

The overwhelming objective is that this book will be a stimulus to encourage a logical scriptural approach to this fascinating prophecy of the Lord Jesus. I am convinced that the principles behind the exposition are sound but I would, to say the least, be naïve if I claimed to have ironed out all the difficulties. I dare to hope that if the principles which underpin the exposition are allowed to influence our approach, not only to the Olivet Prophecy but to prophecy in general, some of the current confusion will be dissipated.

Some may wonder why it has been deemed necessary to include the lengthy appendix on 'realised eschatology'. It fulfils two objectives. It sets out clearly my position with respect to the second coming of Jesus, showing that my conclusions in connection with the Olivet Prophecy in no way detract from a belief in the Lord's future advent. The appendix also will prepare readers for an approach to New Testament prophecy in general to which they are likely to be increasingly exposed as the Realised Eschatology movement gains momentum.

I suggest that the book be first read through ignoring the footnotes and then, perhaps, read again in conjunction with the footnotes, many of which give more extensive information.

John Allfree
Mansfield 2006

CONTENTS

CHAPTER ONE

WHEN SHALL THESE THINGS BE?

Matthew 24

1 And Jesus went out, and
departed from the temple:
and his disciples came to
him for to shew him the
buildings of the temple.
2 And Jesus said unto them,
See ye not all these things?
verily I say unto you, There
shall not be left here one
stone upon another, that
shall not be thrown down.
3 And as he sat upon the
mount of Olives, the
disciples came unto him
privately, saying, Tell us,
when shall these things be?
and what shall be the sign
of thy coming, and of the
end of the world?

Mark 13

1 And as he went out of the
temple, one of his disciples
saith unto him, Master, see
what manner of stones and
what buildings are here!
2 And Jesus answering said
unto him, Seest thou these
great buildings? there shall
not be left one stone upon
another, that shall not be
thrown down. 3 And as he
sat upon the mount of
Olives over against the
temple, Peter and James
and John and Andrew
asked him privately, 4 Tell
us, when shall these things
be? and what shall be the
sign when all these things
shall be fulfilled?

Luke 21

5 And as some spake of the
temple, how it was adorned
with goodly stones and
gifts, he said, 6 As for these
things which ye behold, the
days will come, in the which
there shall not be left one
stone upon another, that
shall not be thrown down.
7 And they asked him,
saying, Master, but when
shall these things be? and
what sign will there be
when these things shall
come to pass?

Background

The nature of the Olivet Prophecy is the more readily appreciated when viewed against the background of certain events in the life of our Lord during the week in which the prophecy was given. These may be enumerated for ease of reference:

1. John 12:1 informs us that six days before the Passover Jesus came to Bethany and, according to verse 12, the next day he went to Jerusalem where the people met him with the cry, "Hosanna: Blessed is the King of Israel that cometh in the name of the Lord." It is Luke who records that at this time the Lord delivered a warning of terrible judgement that was to come upon the people of Israel. He predicted, "The days shall come upon thee, that thine enemies shall cast a trench about thee, and compass thee round, and keep thee in on every side, and shall lay thee even with the ground, and thy children within thee; and they shall not leave in thee one stone upon

another; because thou knewest not the time of thy visitation" (Luke 19:43–44). Having entered the Temple area and "looked round about upon all things" in preparation for the following day's activity, Jesus returned to Bethany for the night (Mark 11:11).

2. The following morning Jesus set out again for Jerusalem and on his way there cursed a fig tree (Mark 11:12–14). We shall return to this incident later; we simply note at this point that this day too, was a day of warning of judgement to come on Israel, for the cursing of the fig tree was, as will be shown in due course, a parable foretelling God's judgement of that fruitless nation. He concluded this day in Jerusalem by entering the Temple area again and forcibly evicting from its precincts those who were buying and selling (Matt. 21:12,13; Mark 11:15–17).

3. The next day was the day of the Olivet Prophecy. What a busy day this was in the ministry of Jesus! And the emphasis throughout was on the impending judgement upon Israel:

   (a) The day began with the chief priests and the elders questioning his authority to teach in God's name. He silenced them with the question about the baptism of John (Mark 11:27-33; Matt. 21:23–27)). He then proceeded to speak to them the parable of the two sons in which his listeners were represented by the son who said that he would work in the vineyard but deceived his father and "went not". The message to these religious leaders of Israel was:

   > "The publicans and the harlots go into the kingdom of God before you. For John came unto you in the way of righteousness, and ye believed him not: but the publicans and the harlots believed him: and ye, when ye had seen it, repented not afterward, that ye might believe him." (Matt. 21:31–32)

   This was the first of a number of stinging rebukes and warnings which Jesus delivered on this day.

(b) He then gave them another parable — the parable of the vineyard (Matt. 21:33–46) — the whole point of which was to warn that "He will miserably destroy those wicked men ... whosoever shall fall on this stone shall be broken: but on whomsoever it shall fall, it will grind him to powder" (vv. 41,44).

(c) Then followed the parable of the marriage of the king's son (Matt. 22:1–14), and again the message of judgement is clear — "When the king heard thereof, he was wroth: and he sent forth his armies, and destroyed those murderers, and burned up their city" (v.7).

(d) Next there is recorded the endeavours of the Herodians, Sadducees and Pharisees to trap him — Is it right to pay tribute (Matt. 22:17)? What about the woman who had seven husbands (v.25)? Which is the greatest commandment (v. 36)? With his devastating answers Jesus silenced his foes. His *coup de grâce* was his question to them, "What think ye of Christ? whose son is he?", which led them to the point where "neither durst any man from that day forth ask him any more questions." Then addressing the people he publicly rebuked their religious leaders — "Woe unto you, scribes and Pharisees, hypocrites!" (23:13 etc.), and then he spelled out the judgement that would come upon them — "Ye serpents, ye offspring of vipers, how shall ye escape the judgement of hell? (i.e. Gehenna[1])...

---

[1] The word translated "hell" here is *géenna* which is the Greek form of the Hebrew, *gay' hinnōm* (= 'the valley of Hinnom') e.g. in Neh. 11:30. "A valley on the west and south of Jerusalem" (G. Abbott-Smith, *A Manual Greek Lexicon of the New Testament*, page 89). This valley figured greatly in the outpouring of God's judgements upon Israel in the Old Testament period. Jeremiah warned the Jews of his day, "The days come, saith the LORD, that it shall no more be called Tophet, nor the valley of the son of Hinnom, but the valley of slaughter: for they shall bury in Tophet, till there be no place. And the carcases of this people shall be meat for the fowls of the heaven, and for the beasts of the earth; and none shall fray them away" (Jer. 7:32,33). This was an extension of the prophecy by Moses in Deuteronomy 28:26 where this kind of language is also used of Israel's judgement. This was fulfilled in the first instance by Nebuchadnezzar king of

that upon you may come all the righteous blood shed on the earth, from the blood of Abel the righteous, unto the blood of Zachariah son of Barachiah, whom ye slew between the sanctuary and the altar" (Matt. 23:33, 35 RV).

(e) It was at this point that he looked upon the city of Jerusalem and, weeping over it, spoke again of impending judgement, saying, "Behold, your house [by which he meant the Temple] is left unto you desolate" (Matt. 23:38).

(f) The attention of the disciples was drawn to the faithful actions of the poor widow casting 'all her living' into the temple collection — a stark contrast to the ostentatious ways of his enemies (Luke 21:1–4). It was about this time that "certain Greeks" presented themselves to Philip requesting that they might see Jesus. This must have been very encouraging to the Lord and he once again pronounced impending judgement on Israel but spoke also of the bringing in of the Gentiles that would soon take place — "Now is the judgment of this world (Gk. *kósmos* = 'the nation of Israel'[2]): now shall the prince of this world be cast out.[3] And I, if I be lifted up from the earth, will draw all men[4] [i.e. Jews and Gentiles] unto me" (John 12:31,32).

Babylon (see Jer. 34:1,20). Jesus was warning that similar judgements awaited the Jews of his day.

2. On this see page 31, footnote 5, where the connection between Israel and *kósmos* is discussed. Further, the form of words — "**this** world" rather than "the world" — confirms that Jesus was referring to that arrangement of things around him — i.e. the nation of Israel.

3. The ruling principle of that system of things was Sin. The death of Jesus would result in Sin's dethronement.

4. It is quite clear from this that Jesus was looking forward to the bringing in of the Gentiles that had been foretold by the Old Testament prophets (e.g. Deut. 32:21 cf. Rom. 10:19; Deut. 32:43 cf. Rom. 15:10; Isa. 42:6-7; Joel 2:32 cf. Rom. 10:12-13). "All men" thus means all nationalities, not every individual. The same teaching is seen in 1 Tim. 2:4 — "God will have all men to be saved, and to come unto the knowledge of the truth." To argue, as some do, that these scriptures teach that God wishes to save every member of the human race is to contradict

It was at this point that the Lord left the temple for the last time (Matt. 24:1). For the best part of three days he had been warning of terrible judgement that was to overtake the nation. The disciples, no doubt to some extent incredulous of many of his words, came to him "to show him the buildings of the temple".

Model of the Temple in the time of Jesus

They were impressed by the beauty of the sanctuary and marvelled at its "goodly stones"[5] (Luke 21:5). His message was

---

the clear scripture teaching that God's purpose is being worked out "according to election" (Rom 9:11; Acts 15:14; 1 Thess. 1:4; etc.) and to misunderstand the purpose of God.

5. Josephus observes that some of these stones were 25 cubits in length, 12 cubits wide and eight cubits high. Using the generally accepted 1 cubit = 18 inches this would mean that some of the stones, all beautifully cut, would measure almost 8,000 cubic feet! (*Antiquities*, 15:11.3).

Josephus did not exaggerate. The temple structure has gone but some idea of the grandeur of the temple may be gauged from the amazing excavations of the Western Wall — part of the supporting wall of the temple platform. The master course "consists of four stones, the longest of which weighs 570 tons and is 44 feet long, ten feet high and 12–16 feet deep! (See photograph on next page). [By the same. The day of judgement was at hand; the house would be made desolate — "There shall not be left here one stone upon another, that shall not be thrown down" (Matt. 24:2).[6]

The excavated master course of the retaining wall of the temple platform contains four stones the largest of which weighs an estimated 570 tons and is 44 feet long, 10 feet high and 12–16 feet deep (see footnote 5)

The Disciples' Questions (Matthew 24:3)

It was this warning of impending judgement that brought the disciples to him as he sat upon the Mount of Olives. They asked him, "Tell us, when shall these things be? and what shall be the sign of thy coming, and of the end of the world?" (Matt. 24:3). Unless this enquiry is placed against the background of the Lord's repeated warning of coming judgement on Jerusalem, and especially his remarks to the disciples about the destruction of the

---

contrast] the largest stone in the Great Pyramid weighs 11 tons." (www.Bibleplaces.com/westernwall.htm.)

[6] Perhaps there is here a reference to the law of "leprosy in a house" (Lev. 14:34 etc.). If the leprosy (a well known scriptural figure for sin) in the house was persistent then the law stipulated that the house was to be broken down, "the stones of it, and the timber thereof" (Lev. 14:45). The presence of them "that sold and bought" and the "tables of the moneychangers" within the temple precincts which, by their actions, they had made "a den of thieves" (Matt. 21:12,13), was an indication of the severity of the leprosy of that house.

Temple, the point of it will not be grasped and the Lord's answer will not be appreciated.

We set out the questions as recorded in Matthew side by side with the parallel verses from Mark and Luke:

MATT. 24:3	MARK 13:4	LUKE 21:7
(1) When shall **THESE THINGS** be?	*(1)* When shall **THESE THINGS** be?	*(1)* When shall **THESE THINGS** be?
(2) What shall be **THE SIGN...**	*(2)* What shall be **THE SIGN...**	*(2)* What **SIGN** will there be...
of thy coming, and of the end of the world?	when all **THESE THINGS** shall be fulfilled?	when **THESE THINGS** shall come to pass?

The enquiry is seen to consist of two questions (not three as is frequently maintained[7]). Failure to accept this very obvious point is the reason for a great deal of confusion in attempts to understand the Lord's answers to the disciples' questions. If we permit ourselves to be guided by the sound principle of allowing scripture to interpret scripture, there is no difficulty in grasping exactly what the disciples were asking.

Question 1 is straightforward. "When shall **these things** be?" is asking when the destruction of the Temple would take place.

Question 2 is the one which presents us with an interesting problem of exposition and which, through a failure to let Mark and Luke explain Matthew, can present unnecessary difficulties. In each of the records they ask about **"the sign"** – it is **the same question** in each gospel account. In Mark and Luke they ask concerning the sign when "these things" (i.e. as in Question 1, the destruction of the temple) will take place. In Matthew they ask, "What shall be the sign of thy coming, and of the end of the world?" This leads to the inescapable conclusion that, in Question 2, the phrase **"these things"** in Mark and Luke, corresponds to **"thy coming, and of the end of the world"** in Matthew. Thus the

[7]. E.g. H. P. Mansfield, *Guidebook to the Gospels*, page 102.

coming of Jesus and the end of the world in Matt. 24:3 has to do with the destruction of the temple and the city of Jerusalem. It will thus now be necessary to demonstrate from the Scriptures that it is correct to speak of Jesus as "coming", at the time of the destruction of Jerusalem, and that this did indeed coincide with "the end of the world".[8]

The Disciples' Unbelief

One point needs to be made before proceeding. It is clear from the gospel records that at the time the Olivet Prophecy was given the disciples did not understand that Jesus had to die, be raised from the dead and ascend to heaven. For example:

1. After their experience on the transfiguration mountain the Lord told them that they were to "tell no man what things they had seen, till the Son of man were risen from the dead." Of their response we read: "They kept that saying with themselves, questioning one with another what the rising from the dead should mean" (Mark 9:9–10).
2. When later Jesus tried to prepare them for what lay ahead he "taught his disciples, and said unto them, The Son of man is delivered into the hands of men, and they shall kill him; and after that he is killed, he shall rise the third day..." The reaction of the disciples was: "...they understood not that saying, and were afraid to ask him" (Mark 9:31–32).

---

[8] At this point I wish to state emphatically my unshakeable belief in the second coming of Jesus to establish God's kingdom on the earth in fulfilment of the covenants made to Abraham and David. It is necessary to emphasise this because there are those who, perhaps because of misunderstanding, have construed the exposition set out in these pages as an attack on these fundamental beliefs. Also it is necessary that we indicate to those who adopt what they describe as a 'realised eschatology' approach to the whole of the New Testament, that a conviction that the Olivet Prophecy was fulfilled in the events surrounding AD 70 does not exclude a belief in a future appearing of the Lord. He will come to restore the nation of Israel as God's kingdom when he will reign on David's throne in Zion according to the covenant made with David (Luke 1:32,33; Acts 3:19–21; Rom. 11:25–27 etc.). See "Realised Eschatology—Is it Sustainable?" on page 120 for greater detail.

3. After the crucifixion of the Lord, when they were confronted by the empty tomb, we are told: "As yet they knew not the scripture, that he must rise again from the dead" (John 20:9).
4. On the road to Emmaus, when Jesus walked with two of them after his resurrection, he chided them (gently, no doubt) saying: "O fools, and slow of heart to believe all that the prophets have spoken: Ought not Christ to have suffered these things, and to enter into his glory?" (Luke 24:25–26).

If they did not understand that he must rise from the dead and ascend to heaven, then it must follow that, whatever they meant when they said, "What shall be the sign of thy coming", they were not asking about what we refer to as the second advent of Jesus. Rather, as will become clear, their question was rooted in the language of the Old Testament prophets and in the teaching of Jesus himself concerning the judgement of a disobedient Israel.[9]

The Old Testament Concept

Two Old Testament references will illustrate the concept of judgement being a divine visitation — a coming of the Lord:

(1) MICAH CHAPTER 1: This chapter concerns the divine judgement, first of the Northern Kingdom of Israel represented by

---

9. It has been maintained (E. Whittaker, *Testimony*, vol. 51, page 65; T. Benson, *Testimony*, vol. 65, page 369; vol. 66, page 44) that the disciples' question — What shall be the sign of thy coming…?" — was in fact triggered by the Lord's words at Matt. 23:39 when he said to Jerusalem, "Ye shall not see me henceforth, till ye shall say, Blessed is ***he that cometh*** in the name of the Lord." It is to this coming, it is argued, that the disciples referred in their question on Mount Olivet.

However, in Matthew 23:39 the phrase "he that cometh" is the Greek *ho erchómenos*, which means, 'the coming one'. This is a way of speaking of Jesus as the Messiah. It is the same phrase used in Matthew 11:3 — "Art thou he that should come, (*ho erchómenos* = 'the coming one') or do we look for another?" For the people of Jerusalem to say, as in Matthew 23, "Blessed is he that cometh in the name of the Lord" was for them to accept Jesus as their Messiah. This was not what the disciples were asking on Mount Olivet. They knew that Jesus was *ho erchómenos*, 'the one that should come' — the Messiah. They were concerned to know when the temple would be destroyed and enquired as to the circumstances that would surround its destruction, as an examination of the questions in the three records shows.

its capital city Samaria, and then of the Southern Kingdom of Judah represented by its capital city Jerusalem:

> "The word of the LORD that came to Micah... which he saw concerning Samaria and Jerusalem... For the transgression of Jacob is all this, and for the sins of the house of Israel. What is the transgression of Jacob? is it not Samaria? and what are the high places of Judah? are they not Jerusalem? Therefore I will make Samaria as an heap of the field... For her wound is incurable; for it is come unto Judah; he is come unto the gate of my people, even to Jerusalem." (Mic. 1:1, 5-6, 9)

The instruments in the hand of God for the judgement of his people were, in the case of Samaria, the power of Assyria, and in the case of Jerusalem, the armies of Assyria in the days of Hezekiah and later the armies of Babylon. However, when the judgements fell upon Israel they are described as a coming of the Lord – "Behold, **the LORD cometh forth** out of his place, and will **come down**, and tread upon the high places of the earth" (Mic. 1:3).

(2) JEREMIAH CHAPTER 4: This also concerns the Babylonian invasion of Judah:

> "I will bring evil from the north, and a great destruction. The lion is come up from his thicket, and the destroyer of the Gentiles is on his way; he is gone forth from his place to make thy land desolate; and thy cities shall be laid waste, without an inhabitant... Destruction upon destruction is cried; for the whole land is spoiled... I beheld the earth, and, lo, it was without form, and void; and the heavens, and they had no light." (Jer. 4:5-7, 20, 23)

There are many similarities between this chapter and the Olivet Prophecy and we shall have reason to refer to it again later. At this point we content ourselves by noting that when the armies of Babylon brought about the desolation described they were but the instrument in God's hand, for it is said that "all the cities thereof were broken down at **the presence of the LORD**, and by his fierce anger" (v. 26).

Thus the Old Testament, when describing the judgement of sinful Israel, speaks of the LORD (Jehovah)) coming against it.

The Teaching of Jesus

Jesus used exactly the same kind of language, teaching that just as Jehovah had come in judgement against Israel in the past, so in the future he (Jesus) would come in judgement against the nation that was about to reject him, for God had "committed all judgment unto the Son" (John 5:22). The following Scriptures, to which brief notes have been appended, will show this.

The Parable of the Wedding Feast (Matt. 22:1–7)

1 And Jesus answered and spake unto them again by parables, and said, 2 The
kingdom of heaven is like unto a certain king, which made a marriage for his son,
3 And sent forth his servants to call them that were bidden to the wedding: and
they would not come. 4 Again, he sent forth other servants, saying, Tell them
which are bidden, Behold, I have prepared my dinner: my oxen and my fatlings
are killed, and all things are ready: come unto the marriage. 5 But they made light
of it, and went their ways, one to his farm, another to his merchandise: 6 And the
remnant took his servants, and entreated them spitefully, and slew them. 7 But
when the king heard thereof, he was wroth: and he sent forth his armies, and
destroyed those murderers, and burned up their city.

1. The king who makes the marriage (v.2) is God.
2. The servants who give the invitation in v.3 represent the prophets until John the Baptist.
3. The "other servants" (v.4) have a different message — "My oxen and the fatlings are killed" — the sacrifice of Jesus, the antitype of the animal sacrifices offered under the law, has happened; "all things are ready". These servants then are the apostles, prophets etc., of the New Testament congregation of believers.
4. Verses 5–6 predict that, just as Israel had rejected the prophets until John the Baptist, so they would reject the apostolic preaching.
5. After his resurrection, Jesus was given "the name" which is above every name (Phil. 2:9 RV), which is the name of

Jehovah[10]. He thus became "the king" of Israel mentioned in verse 7.

6. Thus the king who sends forth his armies to destroy those murderers and burn up their city (v. 7) is the resurrected and glorified Jesus. The Roman armies that destroyed Jerusalem were under the control of Israel's immortal king.

This interpretation is confirmed by Daniel chapter 9, which speaks of the crucifixion of Jesus (v.24) who is referred to as "Messiah the Prince" (v.25). The prophecy then proceeds to speak of the destruction of Jerusalem by the Roman armies, which are styled "The people of the prince" (v.26). The Roman armies were but instruments in Messiah's hands.[11]

The Parable of the Unjust Judge (Luke 18:1–8)

1 And he spake a parable unto them to this end, that men ought always to pray, and not to faint; 2 Saying, There was in a city a judge, which feared not God, neither regarded man: 3 And there was a widow in that city; and she came unto him, saying, Avenge me of mine adversary. 4 And he would not for a while: but afterward he said within himself, Though I fear not God, nor regard man; 5 Yet because this widow troubleth me, I will avenge her, lest by her continual coming she weary me. 6 And the Lord said, Hear what the unjust judge saith. 7 And shall not God avenge his own elect, which cry day and night unto him, though he bear long with them? 8 I tell you that he will avenge them speedily. Nevertheless when the Son of man cometh, shall he find faith on the earth?

1. This parable is set against the background of the Lord's teaching in Luke ch. 17, which is very similar to the Olivet Prophecy (e.g. cf. Luke 17:26 & 37 with Matt. 24:37 & 28). The whole purpose of the parable is to instruct the disciples that

---

10. It is interesting to note that the apostle, in Philippians 2:9–10, appears to be referring to Isaiah 45:23 in which ***Jehovah*** declares, "Unto ***me*** every knee shall bow, every tongue shall swear." The apostle applies this to Jesus. He is able to apply the quotation to the Lord because Jesus had been given "the name" of his Father.

11. Just as the Assyrians were in the hands of God in the Old Testament — "O Assyrian, the rod of mine anger, and the staff in their hand is mine indignation. I will send him against an hypocritical nation, and against the people of my wrath will I give him a charge, to take the spoil, and to take the prey, and to tread them down like the mire of the streets" (Isa. 10:5,6).

when the time of trouble comes, they "ought always to pray, and not to faint" (Luke 18:l).

2. The point of the parable is seen at v.7. The unjust judge avenged the woman; will not God therefore avenge his elect?
3. The elect are the faithful in the ecclesia who will suffer at the hands of the Jews (Matt. 22:6).
4. God did avenge the elect, and it is Luke who tells us precisely **when** they were avenged. The word "avenge" is from the Greek, *ekdikéō*. In the Olivet Prophecy, in Luke 21, the same word is used — "when ye shall see Jerusalem compassed with armies... **these** be the days of vengeance (Gk. *ekdíkēsis*)..." (vv. 20, 22). So the elect were avenged by the Roman armies, as instruments in the Lord's hands, when they besieged Jerusalem in AD 69/70.
5. It should be noted that God was to avenge the elect "speedily" (v. 8), which means exactly what it says,[12] and cannot be stretched to cover nearly 2,000 years of history.
6. This judgement of Israel is spoken of as the Son of man coming against them. In the question, "When the Son of man cometh, shall he find faith on the earth?", the word "earth" in the Greek is *gē*. This word is frequently used to denote the land of Israel (e.g. Matt. 2:6, 20, 21) and there is much evidence in the epistles to show that by the year AD 70, when the Son of man came in judgement against the nation, there was, indeed, widespread apostasy in the Jewish ecclesias.[13]

---

12. The Greek is *en táchei* and is translated "speedily" (AV, RV, RSV and Emph. Diaglott), "quickly" (NIV, Rotherham, Young's Literal).

13. In the Greek, the word "faith" here carries the definite article — **the** faith. Jesus was highlighting the extent of Jewish apostasy that would prevail at the time of the judgement of Jerusalem — "When the Son of man cometh, shall he find the faith in the land?" is the sense of the Lord's question. *The Emphatic Diaglott* translates — "When the Son of man comes, will he find this belief in the land?"

THE LORD'S MOUNT OLIVET PROPHECY

Matthew 10:23

23 But when they persecute you in this city, flee ye into another: for verily I say unto you, Ye shall not have gone over the cities of Israel, till the Son of man be come.

There is little that needs to be said on this verse, which is so clear in its teaching that the work of the disciples would not be finished before Jesus came in judgement against the nation.

Warning to the Sanhedrin (Mark 14:61, 62)

61 But he held his peace, and answered nothing. Again the high priest asked him, and said unto him, Art thou the Christ, the Son of the Blessed? 62 And Jesus said, I am: and ye shall see the Son of man sitting on the right hand of power, and coming in the clouds of heaven.

1. Jesus said to the Sanhedrin that **they** would "see the Son of man sitting on the right hand of power, and coming in the clouds of heaven". It is clear that this cannot refer to what we call the second advent, for it is impossible for the Sanhedrin to be present to witness that. Even if we believe that they are responsible and will be raised from the dead for judgement, they will not see Jesus **"coming"**, for when the dead are raised he has already come (see 1 Thess. 4:16, 17).
2. It should be noted that there is a point of connection here with the Olivet Prophecy, for Jesus is said to come "with the clouds of heaven" (Mark 14:62 RV), which is the language of Matt. 24.30 — "And then shall appear the sign of the Son of man in heaven: and then shall all the tribes of the earth mourn, and they shall see the Son of man **coming in the clouds of heaven** with power and great glory." This will be considered later.[14]
3. The clear teaching of this Scripture then, is that the coming of Jesus as Son of man[15] would be in the lifetime of members of the Sanhedrin.[16]

---

14. *The sign of the Son of man in heaven*, Page 78.

15. This title of Jesus — "the Son of man" — is especially connected with his work as a judge. So John records, "The Father... hath given him authority to execute judgment also, because he is the Son of man." (5:26,27).

The Parable of the Vineyard (Matt. 21:33–41)

33 Hear another parable: There was a certain householder, which planted a
vineyard, and hedged it round about, and digged a winepress in it, and built a
tower, and let it out to husbandmen, and went into a far country: 34 And when the
time of the fruit drew near, he sent his servants to the husbandmen, that they
might receive the fruits of it. 35 And the husbandmen took his servants, and beat
one, and killed another, and stoned another. 36 Again, he sent other servants
more than the first: and they did unto them likewise. 37 But last of all he sent unto
them his son, saying, They will reverence my son. 38 But when the husbandmen
saw the son, they said among themselves, This is the heir; come, let us kill him,
and let us seize on his inheritance. 39 And they caught him, and cast him out of
the vineyard, and slew him. 40 When the lord therefore of the vineyard cometh,
what will he do unto those husbandmen? 41 They say unto him, He will miserably
destroy those wicked men, and will let out his vineyard unto other husbandmen,
which shall render him the fruits in their seasons.

1. The vineyard is Israel (cf. Isaiah ch. 5); the householder (v. 33) is Jehovah; the husbandmen (v.33) are the religious and civil authorities who rejected his servants the prophets (v.35) and who finally killed the householder's son (v. 38) who, of course, is Jesus.
2. The husbandmen said, "This is the heir; come, let us kill him…" (v.38). Jesus was the "heir" and therefore, at his resurrection when he was given "the name that is above every name" (Phil. 2:9 RV and see #5, page 11), he became the Lord of the vineyard.
3. Thus when we read, "When the lord therefore of the vineyard **cometh**" (v.40) to "destroy those wicked men" (v.41), again the idea of Jesus coming in judgement against Israel is being presented.
4. This interpretation is confirmed by verses 42–44, where the coming of the Lord of the vineyard against Israel is spoken of

---

[16] J. Lightfoot confirms this giving the names of some members of the Sanhedrin who were still alive at the time of the destruction of Jerusalem (*Commentary on the New Testament From the Talmud and Hebraica*, vol. 2, page 320). It is interesting to note the words of Stephen to this same Sanhedrin — "Behold, I see the heavens opened, and the Son of man standing on the right hand of God" (Acts 7:56). Was he saying, in effect, that Jesus, who had been exalted to sit at God's right hand, was now, in this act of "standing", preparing to come in judgement against them? — the judgement was near!

as the falling of "the stone which the builders rejected" upon the wicked nation. Jesus was the stone rejected by the builders (cf. Acts 4:11) — they fell on him in crucifying him; he fell on them when he came against them in judgement in AD 69/70.[17]

The End of the World (Matt. 24:3)

This coming of Jesus in judgement, to which the disciples referred in their question, was to be associated with "the end of the world." "What shall be the sign of thy coming, and of the end of the world?" they had asked. There are three different Greek words in Matthew ch. 24 all translated by the one English word "world", and all meaning different things.[18] The word used in v. 3 — "the end of the world" — is *aiōn,* which is correctly rendered in the RV margin as "age". Thus the sense of their enquiry was: "What shall be the sign of thy coming, and of **the end of the age**?"

The destruction of the Temple in AD 70 resulted in the taking away of the daily sacrifice, as predicted in Daniel 8:11, and the end of the Mosaic arrangement. This is why the few years from the time of Jesus to the destruction of Jerusalem are spoken of as "the last days" (e.g. Heb. 1:2).[19]

---

17. There is an interesting connection here with Isaiah ch. 8. For the Jews, Jesus proved to be, as Isaiah predicted, a "stone of stumbling" (Isa. 8:14). The prophet went on to say that, "Many among them shall stumble, and fall..." The extent of their "fall" is seen from the fact that they fell on Jesus in another sense — they arrested him and crucified him. Isaiah continued, "Many... shall... fall, and be broken..." (8:15) — no doubt the words to which Jesus referred when he said, "Whosoever shall fall on this stone shall be broken" (Matt. 21:44). This breaking of the unfaithful nation was the result of Jesus falling on them when he came against them in judgement in AD 69/70.

18. These are: (1) *aiōn*, here in verse 3, which means an age or period of time, as discussed above. (2) *oikouménē*, in verse 14, which refers to the inhabited earth and which in the days of Jesus was the territory of the Roman Empire. (3) *kosmós*, in verse 21, which denotes an ordered arrangement of things. These words will be further discussed at the appropriate places in the exposition.

19. All the writers to the Jewish brethren refer to their days as the last days:

(1) Paul writing to the Hebrews began his letter with the words, "God, who at sundry times and in divers manners spake in time past unto the fathers by the prophets, Hath in ***these last days*** spoken unto us by his Son" (Heb. 1:1–2).

[Footnote continued on next page]

Jesus appeared in the last days of the Mosaic system of things, was rejected, died, and was raised from the dead. He will appear again bringing salvation to them that look for him (Heb. 9:28). There are thus only two appearings of the Lord Jesus. Between these two appearings he is invisibly active in the affairs of men and of nations. The Scriptures teach that shortly after his ascension to heaven he came in judgement against the nation of Israel, brought the Mosaic system to an end by destroying the Temple, and scattered the Jews among the nations of the earth.[20]

It is to this coming in judgement and the ending of the Mosaic age that the disciples referred when they asked Jesus, "Tell us, when shall these things be? and what shall be the sign of thy coming, and of the end of the world?" [21] (Matt. 24:3—"end of the

---

(2) James rebuked the rich, saying, "Ye have laid up your treasure in ***the last days***" (5:3 RV).

(3) Peter, warned of the unfaithful attitude of some, saying, "In ***the last days*** mockers shall come" (2 Pet. 3:3 RV).

(4) Jude, referring to Peter's words, wrote, "Remember ye the words which were spoken before of the apostles of our Lord Jesus Christ; how that they told you there should be mockers in ***the last time***, who should walk after their own ungodly lusts. These be they..." (vv. 17–19) — the mockers were there; the last days had arrived!

(5) John, who wrote later than the others, commented, "Little children, it is ***the last hour:*** and as ye heard that antichrist cometh, even now have there arisen many antichrists; whereby we know that ***it is the last hour***" (1 John 2:18 RV).

[See J. Allfree, *A World Destroyed By Fire*, for greater detail on this point.]

20. It is worth noting that Jesus warned the ecclesias in Ephesus, Pergamos and Sardis that he would "come unto thee quickly" (Rev. 2:5, 16); "as a thief" (3:3); visiting them with judgement, removing their lightstands, unless they repented. Thus the idea of Jesus coming in judgement is not confined to his judgement of Israel.

21. Some (e.g. T. Benson, *Testimony*, vol. 65, page 370) argue that "the end of the world" must refer to the still future advent of the Lord because this is how the words are used in Matthew 13:39,49. This argument is not valid because it begs the question. It assumes that the phrase as used in Matthew 13:39,49 refers to the future advent. This is by no means certain. On the basis of the evidence offered in this exposition with respect to the use of the phrase in Matthew 24 it is more likely that the consummation of the age in Matthew 13 also refers to the end of Judah's Commonwealth. J. Thomas so understood it — "The burning up of the tares has been referred to our far off future! But Jesus said that the tare harvest is συντέλεια τοῦ αἰῶνός, the ending of the Aion: 'As tares are gathered

[Footnote continued on next page]

world" = "consummation of the age?" as in RVm). They desired to know when Jesus would come against the wicked nation of Israel, and destroy the magnificent Temple in Jerusalem.

In the following verses, Jesus therefore presented to them a series of signs, which would indicate that the destruction of Jerusalem was at hand, so that they might be fully prepared to meet the events that were to overtake the nation. These things will be considered in the next five chapters.

---

and burned in the fire, so shall it be in the ending of the Aion. The Son of man shall send forth his agents, and they shall collect out of his kingdom (the Holy Land) all the stumbling blocks, and them doing iniquity, and shall cast them into the furnace of fire: there shall be wailing and gnashing of teeth'… the agents sent were the forces of the Little Horn, 'who severed the wicked from among the just, and cast them into the furnace of fire.' They hemmed up the wicked in the fortified places, especially in Jerusalem. That portion of the Jews who became Judaizers and Gnostics made common cause with the Pharisees against the Roman Eagles… and as they took no heed to the sign, when the Lord of the vineyard sent his Eagles against the state, they were readily ensnared; for instead of fleeing into the mountains, as Jesus advised, they sought refuge in the cities; and thus, as Isaiah predicted, 'they stumbled, and fell, and were broken, and snared, and taken' — Isa. 8:15; Luke 21:35." ("The Last Days of Judah's Commonwealth", *Herald of the Kingdom and Age to Come*, vol. 9, page 152.)

CHAPTER TWO

THE BEGINNING OF SORROWS

Matthew 24

4 And Jesus answered and
said unto them, Take heed
that no man deceive you.
5 For many shall come in
my name, saying, I am
Christ; and shall deceive
many. 6 And ye shall hear of
wars and rumours of wars:
see that ye be not troubled:
for all these things must
come to pass, but the end
is not yet. 7 For nation shall
rise against nation, and
kingdom against kingdom:
and there shall be famines,
and pestilences, and earth-
quakes, in divers places.
8 All these are the
beginning of sorrows.

Mark 13

5 And Jesus answering
them began to say, Take
heed lest any man deceive
you: 6 For many shall come
in my name, saying, I am
Christ; and shall deceive
many. 7 And when ye shall
hear of wars and rumours of
wars, be ye not troubled: for
such things must needs be;
but the end shall not be yet.
8 For nation shall rise
against nation, and king-
dom against kingdom: and
there shall be earthquakes
in divers places, and there
shall be famines and
troubles: these are the
beginnings of sorrows.

Luke 21

8 And he said, Take heed
that ye be not deceived: for
many shall come in my
name, saying, I am Christ;
and the time draweth near:
go ye not therefore after
them. 9 But when ye shall
hear of wars and
commotions, be not
terrified: for these things
must first come to pass; but
the end is not by and by.
10 Then said he unto them,
Nation shall rise against
nation, and kingdom against
kingdom: 11 And great
earthquakes shall be in
divers places, and famines,
and pestilences; and fearful
sights and great signs shall
there be from heaven.

These verses are concerned with the world situation — the political signs of the times — as it would develop during the period leading up to Israel's time of trouble.

Trouble in Israel (Matt. 24:5)

Jesus considered first the nation of Israel itself. "Many shall come in my name, saying, I am Christ" [i.e. the Messiah]. Jesus thus warned his disciples that men would arise claiming to be Israel's promised deliverer. Scripture and profane history unite in testifying to the fact that Jesus' prediction was fulfilled as one false messiah after another arose, promising to deliver the Jews from the Roman yoke:

1. In Acts 5:36 Gamaliel refered to one, "Theudas, boasting himself to be somebody"; and Josephus tells how Theudas led his followers to the river Jordan promising to divide the

waters.[1] Gamaliel also mentions Judas of Galilee who "drew away much people after him" (Acts 5:37).

2. Acts ch. 8 tells us of the activities of Simon:

   > "But there was a certain man, called Simon, which beforetime in the same city used sorcery, and bewitched the people of Samaria, giving out that himself was some great one: To whom they all gave heed, from the least to the greatest, saying, This man is the great power of God." (Acts 8:9–10)

   His claim to be "some great one" appears to have been far more than a claim to be an important man, for the people who accepted his claim proclaimed him to be the "great power of God". Jerome quotes Simon as saying, "I am the word of God, I am the Comforter, I am Almighty, I am all there is of God".[2]

3. Josephus records the situation in Israel under the procuratorships of Felix and Festus, and tells of the repeated emergence of impostors who deluded the multitude, which in a superstitious way was expecting Messiah to come:

   > "These impostors and deceivers persuaded the multitude to follow them into the wilderness, and pretended that they would *exhibit manifest wonders and signs*, that would be performed by the providence of God." [3]

   Josephus refers to them elsewhere adding the information that they claimed to speak by divine inspiration:

   > "There was also another body of wicked men gotten together...These were such men as deceived and deluded the people under *pretence of divine inspiration*, but were for procuring innovations and changes of the government; and these prevailed with the multitude to act like madmen, and went before them *into the wilderness*, as pretending that God would there show them the signal of liberty; but Felix... destroyed a great number of them." [4]

---

1. Josephus, *Antiquities*, 20:5.1. Some have maintained that this is not the same Theudas as in Acts ch. 5. However, it is unlikely that there were two prominent mystic revolutionaries with the same name at around the same time in history.
2. Mansel, *The Gnostic Heresies*, quoted in J. M. Kik, *An Eschatology of Victory*, page 92. F. F. Bruce, *The Book of Acts*, page 178, states, "Irenaeus, (*Against Heresies*, i.23) avers that Simon was the founder of Gnosticism."
3. Josephus, *Antiquities*, 20:8.6.
4. Josephus, *Wars*, 2:13.4.

4. The Egyptian mentioned in Acts 21:38 clearly led astray a great many Jews who were seeking deliverance from Rome. He managed to convince some 4,000 that he was an important prophet, and led them to the Mount of Olives from whence he convinced them he would command the walls of Jerusalem to fall down, enter the city, subdue the Roman authorities there and seize the government of the people.[5]
5. Summarising the situation, J. Moffat writes, "One rival messiah after another, each and all, succeeded more or less in kindling the passions of the people against the Roman Authorities. These popular leaders worked on the religious feeling of the nation. Messianic fanaticism became uncontrollable, and enthusiasts seduced the ardent by semi-political hopes."[6]

World Upheaval

Whilst these things were happening among the Jews, the whole of the Roman Empire was to be in a state of upheaval. There would be:

1. Wars and rumours of wars (Matt. 24:6).[7] Again there is ample historical confirmation that the words of Jesus were fulfilled to the letter. In the land itself there was constant upheaval as the time of judgement drew near. In AD 40 the Roman Emperor, Caligula, ordered an army to march to Jerusalem to place his statue in the temple. The Jews withstood the army and were ready to die to prevent this sacrilege. However, Caligula was assassinated before this could be accomplished and the army withdrew.[8] The incident greatly inflamed revolutionary passions among the Jews who

---

5. Josephus, *Antiquities*, 20:8.6; Eusebius, *Ecclesiastical History*, Bk. 2, Ch. 20. In *Wars* 2:13.5 Josephus says there were 30,000 followers with the Egyptian.

6. In J. Hastings (Editor), *Dictionary of Christ and the Gospels*, Vol. 1, page 574.

7. A very readable account of the history of the period leading up to the destruction of Jerusalem is to be found in N. Faulkner, *Apocalypse: The Great Jewish Revolt Against Rome AD 66-73*.

8. Josephus, *Antiqities* 18:8.1–9; *Wars*, 2:10.1–5; H. H. Ben-Sasson, *A History of the Jewish People*, page 254.

were burdened by crippling taxation and, the lower class at least, struggling to survive.[9]

Things deteriorated during the procuratorship of Cuspius Fadus (AD 44–46) who repressed and harassed the Jews – including the killing of Theudas, the false "messiah" (Acts 5:36).[10] Things came to a head when he antagonised the Jerusalem aristocracy by taking possession of the high priest's garments in order to exert control over the Temple. He was replaced by Tiberius Alexander, a former Jew (AD 46–48), clearly with the idea of calming the very tense situation. However, during the procuratorship of Ventidius Cumanus that followed (AD 48–52), the whole of central Palestine was affected by incidents of communal violence requiring intervention by the Roman military. One was precipitated by a Roman soldier who tore up and burned a copy of the *Torah*. Thousands of irate Jews marched to Caesarea and the procurator was forced to execute the soldier.[11] It was during the rule of Cumanus that "pilgrims from Galilee were attacked by the Samaritans in northern Samaria… Immediately, large numbers of Galileans gathered to fight the Samaritans. Jerusalem was in an uproar. The riots resulted in Roman intervention."[12]

The procuratorships of Antonius Felix (AD 52–60), Porcius Festus (AD 60–62) and Clodius Albinus (AD 62–64) were more measured but the Jews had passed the point of no return in their desire for freedom and revenge. Josephus comments:

> "... deceivers and robbers got together, and persuaded the Jews to revolt, and exhorted them to assert their liberty, inflicting death on those that continued in obedience to the Roman government… they parted themselves into different bodies, and lay in wait up and down the country, and plundered the houses of the great men, and slew the men themselves, and set the

---

9. An excellent and detailed account of the circumstances that spawned the Jewish revolt which led to the destruction of Jerusalem in AD 70 is to be found in Peter L. Osborne, 'Rome Versus Jerusalem: The Great Jewish Revolt and Its Causes', *Testimony*, vol. 74 (2004), page 455; vol. 75 (2005), pages 23, 82, 133 and 162.

10. Josephus, Antiquities, 20:5.1.

11. Josephus, *Antiquities*, 20:5.4.

12. H. H. Ben–Sasson, *A History of the Jewish People*, page 258.

> villages on fire; and this till all Judaea was filled with the effects of their madness." [13]

When Gessius Florus became procurator in AD 64 things were on the brink of irreversible revolution. His method of rulership was the clenched fist, which only aggravated the situation as he continually provoked the Jews. In AD 66 he forcibly took money from the Temple treasury and allowed his soldiers to loot the Upper Market in Jerusalem. This resulted in clashes between the Jews and the Roman soldiers in which many Jews died.[14] It was not long after this that the Jewish zealots attacked a Roman fortress at Masada in which Roman soldiers were killed. They also stopped their obligatory sacrifices for the Emperor (which was a deliberate act of treason) and killed Roman troops in Jerusalem. Josephus actually dates the fateful war, which terminated with the fall of Jerusalem in AD 70, from this act which occurred around AD 66.[15]

In addition to these 'local' events, of which these are but a sample, the whole Roman Empire became increasingly troubled by war and intrigue. Wellesley in his introduction to *Tacitus: The Histories,* which deals with the situation in the Roman Empire in the year AD 69, writes:

> "The year 69—that 'long but single year' as Tacitus earlier called it, offers a wealth of dramatic incident... the vast edifice of the world empire is shaken. Pretender arises against pretender. The frontier armies move on Rome from Spain, Germany, the Balkans and the East. The frontiers themselves are breached by the barbarians. There are palace conspiracies; sudden assassinations, desperate battles; deeds of heroism and perfidy. The scene shifts continuously from one end of the empire to the other, from Britain to Palestine; from Morocco to the Caucasus. Three emperors — Galba, Otho,

---

13. Josephus, *Wars,* 2:13.6.

14. Josephus, *Wars*, 2:14.2; H. H. Ben-Sasson, *A History of the Jewish People*, page 300.

15. Josephus, *Wars*, 2:17.2; *Antiquities,* 20:11.1; S. Grayzel, *A History of the Jews*, page 156; J. Gribetz, et al., *The Timetables of Jewish History*, page 61. See further historical comments on page 39ff.

> and Vitellius meet their end... In all the records of Rome there can scarcely be another year that is so full of calamity."[16]

2. Famines and earthquakes (Matt. 24:7). Again, we need to look no further than the Acts of the Apostles for the fulfilment of the words of Jesus. Acts 11:28 records that there was "a great dearth" over all the Roman world (Gk. *oikouménē*) in the days of Claudius Caesar.[17] That this had a particularly bad effect on Judaea – hence the decision by the brethren in Acts 11:29 to send relief to Jerusalem – is confirmed by Josephus.[18]

Acts 16:26 speaks of the great earthquake that shook the town of Philippi, bringing about the release of Paul and Silas. Further, the earthquake that devastated Pompeii on 5th February, AD 63 is well known,[19] but history also records earthquakes in Crete, Smyrna, Campania, Rome, Judaea, Miletus, Chios, Samos, Laodicea, Colosse and Hierapolis.[20]

3. Fearful sights and great signs from heaven (Luke 21:11). Only Luke mentions these. Even if we allow for the fact that the minds of the historians of those days were influenced by prevailing superstition it is clear that unusual things did take place in the realm of nature. The Jewish historian recounts one such occasion when a force of Idumean soldiers arrived at Jerusalem to assist the Zealots in their political aspirations in AD 68. The soldiers were excluded from the city by the high priest and camped outside the walls:

---

[16] K. Wellesley, *Tacitus:The Histories*, page 9; and see Tacitus, *The Histories*, 1:2, for his own comments on this period.

[17] Bruce comments: "Although there was no single famine affecting the whole empire simultaneously in the reign of Claudius, classical writers testify to the famine conditions which were prevalent in his dominion at various times during his reign. (cf. Seutonius, *Life of Claudius*, xviii. 2; Tacitus, *Annals*, xii. 43; Dio Cassius, *History*, lx. 11; Eusebius, *Chronicle*, Year of Abraham 2065; Orosius, *History*, vii. 6.17)." (F.F. Bruce, *The Book of Acts*, page 243.)

[18] Josephus, *Antiquities*, 3:15.3 and 20:2.5.

[19] Not the eruption of Vesuvius that totally destroyed Pompeii in AD 79. The AD 63 earthquake devastated most of the public buildings and the city was still being rebuilt when the AD 79 disaster struck.

[20] T. Newton, *Dissertations on the Prophecies*, page 335.

"... though in a very bad encampment; for there broke out a prodigious storm in the night, with the utmost violence, and very strong winds, with the largest showers of rain, and continual lightnings, terrible thunderings, and amazing concussions and bellowings of the earth, that was in an earthquake. These things were a manifest indication that some destruction was coming upon men, when the system of the world was put into this disorder; and any one would guess that these wonders foreshewed some grand calamities that were coming." [21]

Tacitus comments on similar occurrences:

"At the close of the year [AD 65 or 66] people talked much about prodigies, presaging impending evils. Never were lightning flashes more frequent, and a comet too appeared, for which Nero always made propitiation..." [22]

Of this same period he wrote:

"A year of shame and of so many evil deeds. Heaven was also marked by storms and pestilence. Campania was devastated by a hurricane, which destroyed everywhere country houses, plantations and crops, and carried its fury to the neighbourhood of Rome, where a terrible plague was sweeping away all classes of human beings..." [23]

The Beginning of Israel's Travail (Matt. 24:8)

Thus Jesus accurately predicted the world situation which was to herald the time of judgement upon the Jews, and he proceeded to say, "These are the beginning of sorrows" (Matt. 24:8). The word "sorrows" is the Gk. *ōdín* = 'travail' (as in RV), thus these political events in Judaea and in the Roman world would mark the beginning of Israel's travail.

There appears to be here a reference to Isaiah ch. 66. This chapter speaks of the work of Jesus, the poor and contrite one who trembled at God's word, who would by his life and death prepare the place of God's rest, and lay the foundation stone of His house (vv.1, 2, cf. John 14:2). At this time when Jesus was among the people of Israel performing his Father's will, the moral state of the nation was as described in vv.3, 4:

---

21. Josephus, *Wars*, 4:4.5.

22. Tacitus, *Annals*, 15:47, quoted by H. Fowler, *The Gospel of Matthew*, vol. 4, page 417.

23. Tactitus, *Annals*, 16:13, quoted by H. Fowler, *The Gospel of Matthew*, vol. 4, page 417.

> "He that killeth an ox is as if he slew a man; he that sacrificeth a lamb, as if he cut off a dog's neck; he that offereth an oblation, as if he offered swine's blood; he that burneth incense, as if he blessed an idol. Yea, **they have chosen their own ways, and their soul delighteth in their abominations.** I also will choose their delusions, and will bring their fears upon them; because when I called, none did answer; when I spake, they did not hear: but they did evil before mine eyes, and chose that in which I delighted not." (Isa. 66:3–4)

The next three verses are intensely interesting from the standpoint of this study, for they comprise a prophetic message designed to give encouragement to the faithful disciples as Israel's judgement drew near:

> "Hear the word of the LORD, ye that tremble at his word; Your brethren that hated you, that cast you out for my name's sake, said, Let the LORD be glorified: but he shall appear to your joy, and they shall be ashamed. A voice of noise from the city, a voice from the temple, a voice of the LORD that rendereth recompence to his enemies. Before she travailed, she brought forth; before her pain came, she was delivered of a man child." (Isa. 66:5–7)

The following points of exposition may be briefly listed:

1. "Your brethren that hated you, that cast you out for my name's sake, said, Let the LORD be glorified" (v.5) describes exactly the attitude of the Jews towards the disciples of Jesus as the destruction of Jerusalem approached. In fact, Jesus himself warned his disciples, "They shall put you out of the synagogues: yea, the time cometh, that whosoever killeth you will think that he doeth God service" (John 16:2). In the Olivet Prophecy itself, Jesus warned his disciples: "They shall lay their hands on you, and persecute you, delivering you up to the synagogues, and into prisons, being brought before kings and rulers for my name's sake" (Luke 21:12).
2. "He shall appear to your joy, and they shall be ashamed" (v. 5). The coming of Jehovah manifest in His Son for the vindication of the faithful and the making ashamed of the wicked nation is the whole burden of the Olivet Prophecy.
3. This rendering of "recompense to his enemies" (v.6) would be Israel's time of travail, but "**before she travailed**, she brought forth; before her pain came, she was delivered of a man child"

(v.7). The man child was Christ. Born of the virgin and declared to be the Son of God with power by the resurrection of the dead, he was the first of Zion's immortal sons, brought forth some 40 years before the travail which culminated in the destruction of AD 70.

We have already had reason to refer to Jeremiah ch. 4 (see page 10). Another point of similarity between the Olivet Prophecy and Jeremiah ch. 4 may be noted here. Speaking of the great destruction which was to overtake the nation of Israel at the hands of the Babylonians, Jeremiah says, "For I have heard a voice as of a **woman in travail,** and the anguish as of her that bringeth forth her first child, the voice of the daughter of Zion, that bewaileth herself, that spreadeth her hands, saying, Woe is me now! for my soul is wearied because of murderers" (Jer. 4:31).

CHAPTER THREE

JEWISH APOSTASY AND GENTILE OPPORTUNITY

Matthew 24

9 Then shall they deliver you up to be afflicted, and shall kill you: and ye shall be hated of all nations for my name's sake. 10 And then shall many be offended, and shall betray one another, and shall hate one another. 11 And many false prophets shall rise, and shall deceive many. 12 And because iniquity shall abound, the love of many shall wax cold. 13 But he that shall endure unto the end, the same shall be saved. 14 And this gospel of the kingdom shall be preached in all the world for a witness unto all nations; and then shall the end come.

Mark 13

9 But take heed to yourselves: for they shall deliver you up to councils; and in the synagogues ye shall be beaten: and ye shall be brought before rulers and kings for my sake, for a testimony against them. 10 And the gospel must first be published among all nations. 11 But when they shall lead you, and deliver you up, take no thought beforehand what ye shall speak, neither do ye premeditate: but whatsoever shall be given you in that hour, that speak ye: for it is not ye that speak, but the Holy Spirit. 12 Now the brother shall betray the brother to death, and the father the son; and children shall rise up against their parents, and shall cause them to be put to death. 13 And ye shall be hated of all men for my name's sake: but he that shall endure unto the end, the same shall be saved.

Luke 21

12 But before all these, they shall lay their hands on you, and persecute you, delivering you up to the synagogues, and into prisons, being brought before kings and rulers for my name's sake. 13 And it shall turn to you for a testimony. 14 Settle it therefore in your hearts, not to meditate before what ye shall answer: 15 For I will give you a mouth and wisdom, which all your adversaries shall not be able to gainsay nor resist. 16 And ye shall be betrayed both by parents, and brethren, and kinsfolks, and friends; and some of you shall they cause to be put to death. 17 And ye shall be hated of all men for my name's sake. 18 But there shall not an hair of your head perish.

At Matthew 24:9, Jesus turned from the political scene to consider the situation prevailing in the congregation of believers. Thus, incidentally, we see that the signs of the times are not all to be sought outside the confines of the ecclesia—a point we should bear in mind when we look at the signs of the times in our day.

Believers Afflicted, Killed, and Hated (Matt. 24:9–10)

Jesus said that the brethren would be called upon to suffer great hardship. They would be "deliver[ed]… up to be afflicted"; they "shall kill you: and ye shall be hated of all nations for my name's sake." The Acts and Epistles show that these words were fulfilled to the letter. Peter and John were imprisoned and threatened (Acts 4); the apostles were imprisoned and beaten by the Sanhedrin (Acts 5); Stephen was stoned (Acts 7); James was killed by Herod who also imprisoned Peter (Acts 12); Saul rampaged through the ecclesias persecuting the brethren, but then became the most persecuted and afflicted of all the Lord's men. (Acts 9; 2 Cor. 11:23–26).

It was not to be at the hands of Jews only that they would receive this treatment. They would be "hated of **all nations**" (v. 9) — a hatred which is evidenced in such Scriptures as Acts 16:19–24, and which reached hideous proportions in the time of Nero in AD 64. The historian Tacitus, writing at the end of the first century some 36 years after the Neronian persecution says:

> "To suppress the common rumour that he had himself set fire to the city [Rome], Nero procured others to be accused, and inflicted exquisite punishments upon those people who were held in abhorrence for their crimes, and were commonly known as Christians... These executions were so contrived as to expose them to derision and contempt. Some were covered over with skins of wild beasts and torn to pieces by dogs; some were crucified; and others having been daubed over with combustible materials, were set up as lights in the night as they burnt to death." [1]

Matthew adds, "Then shall many be offended, and shall betray one another." To illustrate the fulfilment of this we quote again from Tacitus' comments on the Neronian persecution:

> "At first several were seized who confessed, and then by their discovery a great multitude of others were convicted and barbarously executed." [2]

At this point Luke in his account of the Olivet Prophecy records the following words:

> "But before all these, they shall lay their hands on you, and persecute you, delivering you up to the synagogues, and into prisons, being brought before kings and rulers for my name's sake. And it shall turn to you for a testimony. Settle it therefore in your hearts, not to meditate before what ye shall

---

1. Tacitus, *Annals*, quoted by G. Waddington, *A History of the Church*, page 13.

2. Tacitus, *Annals*, 15:44, as quoted by T. Newton, *Dissertations on the Prophecies*.

> answer: For I will give you a mouth and wisdom, which all your adversaries shall not be able to gainsay nor resist." (vv.12–15)

To which Mark, in his record, adds:

> "... whatsoever shall be given you in that hour, that speak ye: for it is not ye that speak, but **the Holy Spirit.**" (Mark 13:11)

This refers to the pouring out of the holy spirit on the believers in the first century, which took place on the day of Pentecost as recorded in Acts ch. 2. This enabled them to witness faithfully for the Lord before the authorities.[3]

Again, the Acts of the Apostles records how these words of Jesus were fulfilled:

1. Acts 4:5–8 records the conflict between Peter and John, and the rulers of Israel: "And when they had set them in the midst, they asked, By what power, or by what name, have ye done this? Then Peter, **filled with the Holy Spirit**, said unto them, Ye rulers of the people, and elders of Israel..." etc.
2. Acts ch. 6 describes a similar dispute between Stephen — "a man full of faith **and of the Holy Spirit**" (v.5) — and those of the synagogue of the Libertines: "Then there arose certain of the synagogue, which is called the synagogue of the Libertines, and Cyrenians, and Alexandrians, and of them of Cilicia and of Asia, disputing with Stephen. And they were not able to resist the wisdom **and the spirit by which he spake.**" (Acts 6:9,10).

---

3. There is here an incidental confirmation that these 'signs of the times' have reference to the days leading up to the events of AD 70. In those days the believers had the ability to speak "as they were moved by the holy spirit". We do not possess this holy spirit gift today. To argue that these words of Jesus in the Olivet Prophecy apply to our days carries with it the corollary that we today can speak by holy spirit, which is manifestly not the case. In this connection it is of more than passing interest to note that when the holy spirit was poured out on the day of Pentecost it is expressly stated that this outpouring took place "in the last days" (Acts 2:17). These were the same "last days" referred to by the apostles when they spoke of the end of Israel under the Law Covenant (see footnote 19, page 16).

False Prophets would Arise (Matt. 24:11)

The ecclesias would be troubled with "many false prophets [that would] rise, and... deceive many" (Matt. 24:11). That false prophets did arise in the Jewish ecclesias as the day of Israel's judgement drew nigh is very clear. Both Paul and Peter joined with Jesus in warning that this would happen:

> "For I know this, that after my departing shall grievous wolves enter in among you, not sparing the flock. Also of your own selves shall men arise, speaking perverse things, to draw away disciples after them." (Acts 20:29,30)

> "But there were false prophets also among the people, even as there shall be false teachers among you, who privily shall bring in damnable heresies, even denying the Lord that bought them, and bring upon themselves swift destruction." (2 Peter 2:1)

Jude and John, who appear to have written their epistles in the few years prior to AD 70,[4] record that these earlier predictions were fulfilled:

> "For **there are** certain men crept in unawares, who were before of old ordained to this condemnation, ungodly men, turning the grace of our God into lasciviousness, and denying the only Lord God, and our Lord Jesus Christ." (Jude 4)

> "Beloved, believe not every spirit, but try the spirits whether they are of God: because many false prophets **are gone out** into the world (Gk. *kosmos*)." [5] (1 John 4:1)

---

4. In my view this is evident from their references to the last days. For textual and historical argument for this early date see J. A. T. Robinson, *Redating the New Testament*, pages 140-199; 254-311; 352.

5. John in his gospel and in the epistles that bear his name uses the word *kósmos* to refer to the nation of Israel. Jesus, whose ministry was to "the lost sheep of the house of Israel" (Matt. 15:24), is said to have come as "a light into the world *(kósmos)*" (John 12:46). He "loved his own [disciples] which were in the world *(kósmos)*" (John 13:1). At his death his disciples would weep and lament but the world *(kósmos)* would rejoice (John 16:20). It was for judgement [poured out in AD 70] that he came into this world *(kósmos)* (John 9:39). It is of this judgement that John writes in his first epistle when he says, "The world *(kósmos)* passeth [Emphatic Diaglott, 'is passing'] away... it is the last hour" (1 John 2:17,18 RV).

A Call to Endurance (Matt. 24: 12,13)

These were difficult days. From outside came the anxieties and pressures of a godless and troubled world; from within there was division and controversy resulting from the activities of the false teachers (cf. 2 Tim. 1:15). For the faithful it was a time of tribulation, which developed in them patience and endurance — "He that shall endure unto the end,[6] the same shall be saved" (Matt. 24:13). But the majority within the ecclesia would become debilitated and spiritually sick: "Because iniquity shall abound, the love of many (Gk. *tōn pollōn* = '**the** many') shall wax cold" (Matt. 24:12). No doubt the same "many" referred to by Peter when, speaking about the apostasy, he says, "**Many** shall follow their pernicious ways; by reason of whom the way of truth shall be evil spoken of" (2 Pet. 2:2).

Thus, there would be signs in the ecclesias, particularly the Jewish ecclesias, both in Palestine and the Diaspora, which would precede the outpouring of the fire of God's judgement on Israel. But before the end came there was to be an outstanding sign of the times.

The Gospel Preached to the Gentiles (Matt. 24:14)

"This gospel of the kingdom shall be preached in all the world for a witness unto all nations; and then shall the end come," said Jesus. "The end" in the context, is "the end of the age" mentioned in the disciples' question in verse 3. Thus Jesus was telling his disciples that before the destruction of the city and temple, the gospel had to be "preached in all the world". The word "world"

[6] "The end" here is that "end" referred to by the disciples in their question in Matt. 24:3 — the end of the age. There can be no doubt that those who were faithful in that day of severe trial will be saved in the ultimate sense. But it appears that Jesus here is speaking of being saved from the Roman holocaust. In Luke's account he says, "There shall not an hair of your head perish" (Luke 21:18). We shall see when we come to consider Matt. 24:15–19 that the faithful, in obedience to the words of Jesus, fled Judaea and were saved.

here is the Gk. *oikouménē* and denotes 'the inhabited earth' [7]— the known Roman world.[8]

Doubtless, when Jesus said, "But he that shall endure unto the end, the same shall be saved", the disciples would have been reminded of an earlier occasion, when Jesus said a very similar thing:

> "And ye shall be hated of all men for my name's sake: but he that endureth to the end shall be saved" (Matt. 10:22).

In fact there is an interesting parallel between Matthew ch. 24 and Matthew ch. 10 in connection with the bringing in of the Gentiles, which can be set out as follows:

MATTHEW 10	MATTHEW 24
"And the brother shall deliver up the brother to death, and the father the child: and the children shall rise up against their parents, and cause them to be put to death." (v. 21)	"And then shall many be offended, and shall betray one another, and shall hate one another." (v. 10)
"But ***he that endureth to the end*** shall be saved." (v. 22)	"But ***he that shall endure unto the end***, the same shall be saved." (v. 13)
"Ye shall not have gone over the cities of Israel, ***till the Son of man be come.***" (v. 23)	"And this gospel of the kingdom shall be preached in all the world for a witness ***unto all nations;*** and ***then shall the end come.***" (v. 14)

These two accounts describe two separate preaching missions — in Matthew ch. 10, to the Jews and in Matthew ch. 24, to the Gentiles. The apostles who were preaching to the Gentile world would actually accomplish the work of witnessing to all nations before the end came. But not so those who were preaching to the Jews — their ministry was to be interrupted by the coming of the Son of man.

---

7. G. Abbott-Smith, *Manual Greek Lexicon of the New Testament*, page 313.

8. The *oikouménē* of the time of Jesus and the apostles was that world of which we read in Luke 2:1 — "It came to pass in those days, that there went out a decree from Caesar Augustus, that all the world *(oikouménē)* should be taxed" — i.e. the territories of the Roman Empire.

This emphasises the great difficulties that the apostles who were sent to the circumcision were to face in the first century. Whilst there were many Gentiles ready and eager to accept the word of salvation, the Jews were hardhearted and stubborn, and rejected the truth — so much so that the gospel was preached in the entire Roman Empire before it reached every city in Israel. The attitude of the Jews towards the gospel message is illustrated by the words of Paul who, on one occasion, said to a congregation of typically hardhearted Jews, "It was necessary that the word of God should first have been spoken to you: but seeing ye put it from you, and judge yourselves unworthy of everlasting life, lo, we turn to the Gentiles" (Acts 13:46).

Jesus, then, prophesied that before the end came, the gospel would be preached in Gentile lands. In doing so, he endorsed the predictions of the earlier prophets. For example, Moses in Deuteronomy ch. 32 gave the same sequence of events:

1. Of Israel God says, "I will see what **their end** shall be" (v.20).
2. Before the end comes he says, "I will move them [Israel] to jealousy with those which are not a people" (v.21). Paul quotes this in Romans 10:19 and applies it to the bringing in of the Gentiles taking place in New Testament times.
3. Then follows the prophetic description of the end of the nation of Israel. "For a fire is kindled in mine anger, and shall burn unto the lowest hell, and shall consume the earth with her increase, and set on fire the foundations of the mountains" (v.22) — language that finds its echo in 2 Peter 3:10 (see comments on page 70).

The fulfilment of this prediction of Jesus is described in the New Testament records of the apostolic labours especially in the book of Acts. The conversion of some Jews "out of every nation under heaven" (Acts 2:5) marked the start of this movement towards the Gentiles. These Jews who were at Jerusalem for the feast of Pentecost returned to their homes where, no doubt, they became nuclei of new ecclesias in those places, thus preparing the way for the future spreading of the gospel in those areas. Speaking of this preaching activity of the apostles, prophets, and evangelists, Paul, applying the words of Psalm 19, comments, "Their sound went into all the earth, and their words unto the ends of the world (Gk. *oikouménē*)" (Rom. 10:18). That great preacher to the Gentiles summarises this work when he says, "The gospel... was preached to every creature which is under heaven" (Col. 1:23).

Newton's comments on this are worth quoting.

> "Clement, who was a contemporary and fellow labourer with St. Paul, says of him in particular, that he was a preacher both in the east and in the west, that he taught the whole world righteousness, and travelled as far as the utmost border of the west: and if such were the labours of one apostle, though the chiefest of the apostles, what were the united labours of them all? It appears, indeed, from the writers of the history of the church, that before the destruction of Jerusalem the gospel was not only preached in Lesser Asia, and Greece, and Italy, the great theatres of action then in the world; but was likewise propagated as far northward as Scythia, as far southward as Ethiopia, as far eastward as Parthia and India, as far westward as Spain and Britain... Eusebius informs us, that the apostles preached the gospel in all the world; and that some of them passed beyond the ocean to the Britannic Isles. Theorodet likewise affirms, that the apostles had induced every kind of men to embrace the gospel, and among the converted nations he reckons particularly the Britons." [9]

There can be no doubt that the gospel was preached to all nations in the Roman world before AD 70, and the way of salvation was thus opened to the Gentiles. This great transition in the purpose of God was consolidated when the nation of Israel, with its temple, was destroyed.[10]

---

9. T. Newton, *Dissertations on the Prophecies*, page 341.

10. A number of expositors apply Matthew 24:14 to the preaching activities of believers in modern times. One suggestion is that it refers to the work of the Bible Societies in making the Scriptures available in different languages (H. N. Sargent, *The Marvels of Bible Prophecy*, page 375; A. Hayward, *Great News for the World*, page 16; E. Whittaker, *Testimony*, vol. 51, page 138). Others maintain that it has to do with overseas preaching and that Jesus will not return until the Truth has been preached in all nations of the modern world (e.g. D. Heaster, *Beyond Bible Basics*, page 313; *The Last Days*, page 153). I have myself been involved in overseas preaching and have no desire to discourage this important activity. But I believe that Matthew 24:14 has reference to the apostolic labours in the Roman Empire.

CHAPTER FOUR

THE ABOMINATION OF DESOLATION

Matthew 24

15 When ye therefore shall
see the abomination of
desolation, spoken of by
Daniel the prophet, stand in
the holy place, (whoso
readeth, let him understand:)
16 Then let them which be in
Judaea flee into the
mountains: 17 Let him which
is on the housetop not
come down to take any
thing out of his house:
18 Neither let him which is in
the field return back to take
his clothes. 19 And woe unto
them that are with child, and
to them that give suck in
those days! 20 But pray ye
that your flight be not in the
winter, neither on the
sabbath day.

Mark 13

14 But when ye shall see the
abomination of desolation,
spoken of by Daniel the
prophet, standing where it
ought not, (let him that
readeth understand,) then
let them that be in Judaea
flee to the mountains:
15 And let him that is on the
housetop not go down into
the house, neither enter
therein, to take any thing
out of his house: 16 And let
him that is in the field not
turn back again for to take
up his garment. 1 But woe
to them that are with child,
and to them that give suck
in those days! 18 And pray
ye that your flight be not in
the winter.

Luke 21

20 And when ye shall see
Jerusalem compassed with
armies, then know that the
desolation thereof is nigh.
21 Then let them which are
in Judaea flee to the
mountains; and let them
which are in the midst of it
depart out; and let not them
that are in the countries
enter thereinto. 22 For these
be the days of vengeance,
that all things which are
written may be fulfilled.

At Matthew 24:15 Jesus began to give to his disciples more detailed information concerning the actual time of the end, and advice as to what they should do. "When ye[1] therefore shall see the abomination of desolation, spoken of by Daniel the prophet, stand in the holy place [2]… then let them which be in Judaea flee into the mountains."

---

1. Note carefully to whom Jesus was speaking. Those disciples would see the abomination of desolation. We only create difficulties of exposition by ignoring to whom and of whom Jesus was speaking.

2. The "holy place" is a translation of the Greek *tópō hagiō*. The word *tópos*, in the plural form, has already been used in Matthew 24:7 — "famines… and earthquakes, in divers places *(tópous)*." The word denotes 'a region or locality'. Clearly in Matthew 24:15 it does not refer to the Holy Place in the Temple. Whilst it is true that the Romans did desecrate the Temple as reported by Josephus (*Wars*, 6:6.1), by the time this had happened it would have been too late for the disciples to obey the words of Jesus to "flee to the mountains". The *Emphatic Diaglott* renders *tópō hagiō* here as "holy ground". Allowing Luke to interpret

[Footnote continued on next page]

There are four references in Daniel to this abomination of desolation:

1. Daniel 8:11–13

"Yea, he magnified himself even to the prince of the host, and by him the daily sacrifice was taken away, and the place of his **sanctuary was cast down.** And an host was given him **against the daily sacrifice** by reason of transgression, and it cast down the truth to the ground; and it practised, and prospered. Then I heard one saint speaking, and another saint said unto that certain saint which spake, How long shall be the vision concerning the daily sacrifice, and **the transgression of desolation,** to give both the sanctuary and the host to be trodden under foot?"

Here we read of the little horn of the goat, which can be shown to refer to the power of Rome, described as "the transgression of desolation"[3] or "the transgression that maketh desolate" (RV).[4]

2. Daniel 11:31

"And arms shall stand on his part, and they shall pollute **the sanctuary** of strength, and shall **take away the daily sacrifice,** and they shall place the **abomination that maketh desolate.**"

Matthew, "the abomination of desolation... in the holy place" (Matt. 24:15), corresponds to "Jerusalem compassed with armies" (Luke 21:20). Thus the holy place referred to is Jerusalem. The time referred to would appear to be that when Cestius Gallus attacked Jerusalem in AD 66. (See pages 23ff & 39ff.)

[3] "The transgression of desolation" here refers no doubt to Israel's transgression (v. 12), and the "desolation" to that to be visited upon Israel by the Roman little horn, elsewhere referred to as "the abomination that maketh desolate".

[4] The four horns on the Grecian goat (Dan. 8:8,22) which arose after the death of Alexander the Great represented the four generals — Cassander, Lysimachus, Seleucus and Ptolemy — who carved up the empire between them. Two of these are important from the standpoint of Scripture — the empires of Seleucus and Ptolemy, which in Daniel 11 become known as the king of the north and the king of the south. The power of Rome emerged on the territory of Alexander's empire when it conquered Syria in BC 65. It was at this point that it became the little horn, arising out of the Seleucid horn of the goat. Of this little horn we are told that: (1) It "waxed exceeding great... toward the pleasant land" (which it did, taking Judaea in BC 63); (2) It "magnified [itself] even to the prince of the host" (which it did when it crucified Jesus); (3) It would take away the daily sacrifice and cast the Temple to the ground (which Rome did in AD 70) (Dan. 8:9–11).

This passage has to do with a power referred to as "the ships of Chittim" (v. 30) that would come against the King of the North (Antiochus Epiphanes, see footnote 4) when he invaded Egypt and was about to take Alexandria. The ships of Chittim carried the Roman military officials who had responded to a request from the Egyptian monarch. They demanded, and secured, the return of Antiochus to Syria. Many expositors consider that the "abomination that maketh desolate" in this passage refers to Antiochus himself who, returning to Syria, vented his rage on the Jews. However, it is more likely that the reference is to the Romans who were soon to conquer Syria and occupy the Holy Land. It was they who eventually, in AD 70, removed the daily sacrifice and showed themselves to be "the abomination that maketh desolate".

3. Daniel 9:26, 27

"And after threescore and two weeks shall Messiah be cut off, but not for himself: and the people of the prince that shall come shall **destroy the city and the sanctuary;** and the end thereof shall be with a flood, and unto the end of the war **desolations** are determined. And he shall confirm the covenant with many for one week: and in the midst of the week he shall cause **the sacrifice and the oblation to cease,** and **for the overspreading of abominations he shall make it desolate** [RV shall come **one that maketh desolate**], even until the consummation, and that determined shall be poured upon the desolate."

Here we read of the "people of the prince"[5] described as "one that maketh desolate" (RV) for they would "destroy the city and the sanctuary" — a clear reference to the power of Rome.

4. Daniel 12:11

"From the time that the **daily sacrifice shall be taken away,** and the **abomination that maketh desolate** set up, there shall be a thousand two hundred and ninety days."

---

[5] In the context "the prince" is "Messiah the prince" (9:25). In which case, speaking of the Roman armies as "the people of the prince that shall come" to destroy the city and the sanctuary, reminds us of the Parable of the Wedding Feast (see page 11) when "the king", being filled with indignation against the people who ignored his invitation, "sent forth ***his armies*** and destroyed those murderers and burned up their city" (Matt. 22:7).

> From the standpoint of this study we simply note that this confirms the association between the power described as "the abomination that maketh desolate" and the taking away of the daily sacrifice — which Rome did in AD 70.

Confirmation that each of these verses is indeed speaking about the same power, the power of Rome, comes from noting that in each of these references there is mention made of the ending of the Mosaic system by the destruction of the Temple and the taking away of the daily sacrifice. The Lord gives his own confirmation of this exposition when in the parallel record in Luke 21 we are told, "When ye shall see Jerusalem compassed with armies, then know that **the desolation** thereof is nigh" (v. 20). Thus the armies of Rome, standing on the holy ground of God's land, constituted the abomination of desolation.

The presence of the abomination of desolation in the land of Israel was to be the signal for the faithful to flee the land of Judaea. They were to leave in haste at the first signs of the Roman legions.[6]

Things started to move in the year AD 66. It was in that year, as previously noted,[7] that Gessius Florus, the Roman procurator of Judaea, stole 17 talents of sacred money from the Temple treasury. This led to serious conflict between him and the Jews and there was, in consequence, a great deal of bloodshed, both of Jews and Romans. The situation, carefully orchestrated by the Jewish Zealots, developed into a wholesale revolt against Rome. Gessius

---

6. Jesus instructed his disciples to pray that this departure would not be "in the winter, neither ***on the sabbath day***" (Matt. 24:20). This reference to the sabbath day again fixes the prophecy to Israel and in particular to those days leading up to the destruction of Jerusalem. There were believers amongst the Jews who continued to "[esteem] one day above another" and who observed "days, and months" (Rom. 14:5; Gal. 4:10), and only when they sought to impose this on others as a condition of salvation were they condemned. A flight on the sabbath would have been inconvenient for other reasons too. Such activity on the sabbath, which would have involved more than "a sabbath day's journey" (cf. Acts 1:12) in the midst of the conditions then prevailing would have been to invite death from their own people.

7. Page 23.

Florus eventually had to concede that the situation was beyond his control and fled, so that it was necessary for the legate of Syria, Cestius Gallus, to intervene. He marched south with the Twelfth Legion, and other forces drafted in for the occasion, with the objective of recapturing Jerusalem from the rebels. Having besieged Jerusalem he was unable to take the city easily, misjudged the situation, and withdrew. Josephus comments:

> "When Cestius was **come into the city,** he set the part called Bezetha… on fire; as he did also to the timber market: after which he came into the upper city, and pitched his camp over against the royal palace; and had he at this very time attempted to get within the walls by force, he had won the city presently, and the war had been put an end to at once… It then happened that Cestius was not conscious either how the besieged despaired of success, nor how courageous the people were for him; and so he recalled his soldiers from the place, and by despairing of any expectation of taking it, without having received any disgrace, he returned from the city **without any reason in the world.**" [8]

As he marched north, away from Jerusalem, in November of AD 66, his army was ambushed by the Jews at the pass of Beth-horon with the loss of some 6,000 men. This greatly encouraged the Jewish Zealots in their quest for liberation from Rome.

In AD 67, Nero, appreciating the seriousness of the situation, sent Vespasian with his son Titus with the Eastern legions to sort out the Jews. Meanwhile the faithful took advantage of the situation and, in obedience to the Lord's command, fled the city. Eusebius records that the believers "in accordance with a certain oracle" removed from Jerusalem, and went to Pella, a city of Peraea.[9]

Vespasian

Vespasian's highly organised army began its work in Galilee, ruthlessly destroying Gadara, Jotapata, Joppa, Tiberias, Gamala, and other smaller towns.

---

8. Josephus, *Wars*, 2:19.4,7.

9. J. Stevenson, *A New Eusebius*, page 6.

Meanwhile, during the winter of AD 67/68 the situation in Jerusalem was desperate with three warring factions murdering and plundering the inhabitants. John of Gischala, who had fled before Vespasian in Galilee in November AD 67, became leader of the Zealot party in Jerusalem. He was opposed to what we might call the 'moderate peace party' — those who wanted to reach accommodation with Rome — and murdered some of the city's most illustrious inhabitants. A contingent of Idumaeans (considered to be half-Jews) had also entered the fray, ostensibly to support the Zealots, but in fact they pursued their own agenda of robbery and violence. Eventually the Idumaeans could not come to terms with the excesses of the Zealots and left the city leaving John of Gischala as the undisputed potentate of Jerusalem.

Having put down the rebellion in Galilee the Roman generals wanted Vespasian to attack the capital but he thought it prudent to leave the warring factions to weaken themselves and he directed his attention elsewhere. By the end of spring AD 68 Vespasian had crushed all opposition, not only in Galilee but also in Peraea, western Judaea and Idumaea, and was at last preparing to approach Jerusalem. Then, hearing of the suicide of the Roman Emperor Nero, once more he postponed his attack on the city, giving any hesitating believers one last opportunity to flee. Nero was succeeded by Galba, but he was murdered in January AD 69 at the instigation of Otho who took the throne but only reigned until April when he committed suicide rather than face civil war against his rival Vitellius. Vitellius had been proclaimed emperor by the army in Germany while Galba was still reigning, but only lasted until December AD 69, when he too was murdered.

Meanwhile, Simon bar Giora (= son of a proselyte) rampaged through Idumaea and southern Palestine pillaging and plundering and raising a revolutionary army. He was regarded by his followers and also by the Romans as the most serious would-be 'king of the Jews'.[10] Vespasian thought it necessary to march south and so was again diverted from attacking Jerusalem. Simon

10. N. T. Wright, The New Testament and the People of God, page 177.

marched to Jerusalem and entered the capital with his 'army' aggravating the situation there. There were now two tyrants in the city, fighting each other and oppressing the citizens of Jerusalem.

Vitellius was accepted as Emperor by the Senate in April 69 but he was an unpopular choice, particularly with the legions of Egypt, Syria and Palestine, who proclaimed Vespasian emperor. In December AD 69 Vitellius was murdered and Vespasian departed for Rome leaving Titus in command. Titus prepared to restart the siege.[11]

Titus

Titus arrived at Jerusalem in April AD 70. Inside the city the warring factions had set fire to the stores of grain that were intended to support them during the siege. Just before the final siege began, in spite of the civil war in Jerusalem and the presence of the Roman armies, Jews flocked into Jerusalem in their thousands to keep the Passover.

The siege commenced. "Woe unto them that are with child, and to them that give suck in those days!" said Jesus (Matt. 24:19). It was the most dreadful siege of history. In order to survive the Jews were compelled to eat unclean animals, leather girdles and shoes and even their own children—as had been predicted in Deuteronomy 28:53:

> "And thou shalt eat the fruit of thine own body, the flesh of thy sons and of thy daughters, which the LORD thy God hath given thee, in the siege, and in the straitness, wherewith thine enemies shall distress thee."

---

[11] The various accounts of this period are largely based on the writings of Josephus especially, *Wars*, book 4:9–11 and also book 5. For details see, for example, H. H. Milman, *The History of the Jews*, page 374 etc.; F. F. Bruce, *Israel and the Nations*, page 222, but especially Emil Schürer, *A History of the Jewish People in the Time of Jesus Christ*, div. 1, vol. 2, pages 207–247. There is a summary of the history of this time in R. Roberts, *The Ways of Providence*, pages 285–325.

Josephus recounts a very gruesome story about a woman who boiled her son and then ate him in two meals.[12]

Such were the dreadful calamities that were to overtake the Jewish nation. Well might Jesus describe those days as a time of "great tribulation, such as was not since the beginning of the world to this time, no, nor ever shall be" (Matt. 24:21).[13]

The Arch of Titus in Rome built to celebrate the fall of Jerusalem in AD 70.

The Days of Vengeance (Luke 21:22)

In Luke's account, Jesus adds at this point, "For these be the days of **vengeance**, that all things which are written may be fulfilled"

12. Josephus, *Wars*, 6:3.4.

13. On this verse see page 47ff.

(Luke 21:22). Jesus' allusion here to one of his earlier parables, the parable of the unjust judge in Luke 18:1–8, has already been noted. The salient points of this parable may be repeated as follows:

1. The unjust judge avenged the widow of her adversary lest by her continual coming she weary him.

2. God, the righteous judge, was to speedily avenge (Gk. *ekdikéō*) the elect of their adversaries.

3. This vengeance would be meted out when the Son of man came in judgement against them. A visitation that was mediated through the Roman armies.

4. At that time, a state of Jewish ecclesial apostasy would prevail: to the point where it is asked, "Shall he find [the] faith on the earth?" (Gk. *gē* = 'land', i.e. the land of Israel).

When Jesus referred to this avenging (Gk. *ekdikéō*) of the elect in the Olivet Prophecy, he said, "These be the days of vengeance (Gk. *ekdíkēsis*), that **all things which are written** may be fulfilled". It ought, therefore, to occasion no surprise to find that the parable of the unjust judge has its basis in Old Testament prophecy, and in particular Deuteronomy ch. 32.

Deuteronomy 32: This chapter has already been seen to have connections with AD 70. Consider also the following:

1. God is spoken of as a judge: "For the LORD shall **judge his people,** and repent himself for his servants" (v. 36).

2. It speaks of vengeance against the Truth's adversaries: "To me belongeth **vengeance** (the LXX here has *ekdíkēsis*), and recompence; their foot shall slide in due time" (v. 35).

3. This vengeance was to be effected speedily: "For the day of their calamity is at hand, and the things that shall come upon them **make haste**"(v. 35).

It is also interesting to observe that Deuteronomy ch. 32 is quoted in Hebrews 10:30. Hebrews ch. 10 has much to do with AD 70 and the events surrounding it, and deserves consideration.

Hebrews 10: This chapter must be examined in the light of the situation that existed in the ecclesias in the first century. The early ecclesias were troubled from the outset by those who desired to return to the keeping of the Law of Moses as a means of salvation — the Judaizers. The Judaizing tendency was particularly strong, as would be expected, within the Hebrew ecclesias in the land of Judaea. Much of the epistle to the Hebrews is, therefore, devoted to dealing with this particular problem, and in chapter 10 the apostle seeks to show that to return to the Law was a serious apostasy from the truth in Christ.

1. He points out that the Mosaic sacrifices could never provide true and lasting forgiveness of sins — they could never "make the comers thereunto perfect" (v. 1).

2. He speaks of Jesus as the true sin offering: "But this man, after he had offered one sacrifice for sins for ever, sat down on the right hand of God" (v. 12).

3. He describes those who sin wilfully — in the context surely a reference to those who were turning back to the Law as the means of salvation — and says, "If we sin wilfully after that we have received the knowledge of the truth, there remaineth **no more sacrifice for sins**" (v. 26).

4. These wilful sinners — the Judaizers — are warned of the judgements soon to overtake them: "He that despised Moses' law died without mercy under two or three witnesses: Of how much sorer punishment, suppose ye, shall he be thought worthy, who hath trodden under foot the Son of God?" (vv. 28,29).

5. Quoting from Deuteronomy ch. 32 he then warns the Judaizers that God — the Righteous Judge — will execute vengeance upon them: "For we know him that hath said, **Vengeance** (Gk. *ekdíkēsis*) **belongeth unto me**, I will

recompense, saith the Lord. And again, **the Lord shall judge his people**" (v. 30).

6. This judgement will take place speedily, at the coming of the Son of man: "For yet **a little while**, and he that shall come will come, and **will not tarry**"[14](v. 37).

And indeed, the Son of man did come speedily, and execute vengeance [15] upon the adversaries of the Truth. The result was that Israel suffered "great tribulation, such as was not since the beginning of the world to this time, no, nor ever shall be" (Matt. 24:21).

---

14. "For yet a little while" appears to be a reference to Haggai 2:6 — "Yet once, it is a little while, and I will shake the heavens, and the earth..." In Hebrews 12:27 the apostle refers to these words again, commenting, "...Yet once more, signifieth the removing of those things that are shaken, as of things that are made, that those things which cannot be shaken may remain." The "heavens and the earth" which were shaken and removed are, together, a scriptural figure of the nation of Israel as organised under the Mosaic Law Covenant concerning which, in Hebrews 8:13, the apostle has already stated that it "decayeth and waxeth old [and] is ready to vanish away". Of these heavens and earth more will be said in our consideration of Matthew 24:29.

"He that shall come will come, and will not tarry" is a quotation from Habakkuk 2:3. As earlier noted (page 8, footnote 9) the phrase "He that shall come" (Gk. *ho erchómenos* = 'the Coming One') is used elsewhere as a title of Messiah. The words simply mean 'In a very little while the Messiah will arrive and delay no longer'.

Thus here, in Hebrews 10:37, is another example of the belief of the apostles that Jesus was soon ("in a very little while" RV) to come and bring an end to the Mosaic arrangement. This coming was to be by manifestation in the Roman armies as we have shown.

15. Another reference to this "vengeance" occurs in Isaiah 61:1–2. This looks forward to the ministry of Jesus — "The Spirit of the Lord GOD is upon me; because the LORD hath anointed me to preach good tidings unto the meek; he hath sent me to bind up the brokenhearted, to proclaim liberty to the captives, and the opening of the prison to them that are bound; To proclaim the acceptable year of the LORD, and the day of vengeance of our God..." When Jesus read this scripture in the synagogue at Nazareth he stopped at the words "to proclaim the acceptable year of the LORD", sat down and said, "This day is this scripture fulfilled in your ears" (Luke 4:18–21). He did not read "and the day of vengeance of our God" because that was not fulfilled at that time; its fulfilment was some 40 years hence.

CHAPTER FIVE

THE GREAT TRIBULATION

Matthew 24

21 For then shall be great
tribulation, such as was not
since the beginning of the
world to this time, no, nor
ever shall be. 22 And except
those days should be
shortened, there should no
flesh be saved: but for the
elect's sake those days
shall be shortened.

Mark 13

19 For in those days shall be
affliction, such as was not
from the beginning of the
creation which God created
unto this time, neither shall
be. 20 And except that the
Lord had shortened those
days, no flesh should be
saved: but for the elect's
sake, whom he hath
chosen, he hath shortened
the days.

Luke 21

23 But woe unto them that
are with child, and to them
that give suck, in those
days! for there shall be
great distress in the land,
and wrath upon this people.
24 And they shall fall by the
edge of the sword, and shall
be led away captive into all
nations: and Jerusalem
shall be trodden down of
the Gentiles, until the times
of the Gentiles be fulfilled.

At the time when the abomination of desolation stood in the holy place and the faithful had fled to the mountains, **"then"** (Mk. **"in those days"**) there would be "great tribulation" (Gk. *thlípsis megálē*).

The word "tribulation" (Gk. *thlípsis*) is the word used in the LXX translation of Deuteronomy ch. 28 concerning the siege of Jerusalem — "Thou shalt eat the fruit of thine own body… in the siege, and in the **straitness** (LXX, *thlípsis* = 'tribulation')" (v. 53, also vv. 55, 57). The phrase "great tribulation" also occurs in Jeremiah 11:16 LXX, where the prophet speaks of this same judgement of Israel as that which forms the substance of the Lord's Mount Olivet Prophecy. Addressing Israel, Jeremiah says, "The LORD called thy name, a green olive tree, fair, and of goodly fruit: with the noise of a **great tumult** he hath kindled fire upon it" (v. 16). In the LXX the phrase "great tumult" is, in the Greek, *megálē hē thlípsis* (Lit., 'the great tribulation'). Interestingly, having in this verse described Israel as "a green olive tree", Jeremiah proceeds to say, "the branches of it are broken" (v. 16). Paul takes this up in Romans ch. 11, and applies it to the bringing in of the Gentiles — that great sign of the times (to which, as we have seen, the Lord directed his disciples in Matthew 24:14):

> "And if some of the branches be broken off, and thou (i.e. Gentiles), being a wild olive tree, wert graffed in among them, and with them partakest of the root and fatness of the olive tree; Boast not against the branches... because of unbelief they were broken off, and thou standest by faith... If God spared not the natural branches (Israel), take heed lest he also spare not thee." (Rom. 11:17–21).

The "great tribulation" was the siege of AD 69/70, and the associated carnage throughout Palestine, as discussed in chapter 4. For the Jews of Palestine, and especially of Jerusalem, it was indeed a time of trouble such as never was and never will be again.[1, 2] For what it is worth, this was the opinion of the observer, Josephus:

> "It is therefore impossible to go distinctly over every instance of these men's iniquities. I shall, therefore, speak my mind here at once briefly — That neither did any other city ever suffer such miseries, nor did any age ever breed a generation more fruitful in wickedness than this was, from the beginning of the world." [3]

---

1. Some may feel disposed to question this, arguing that the future invasion of Israel by the power from the north (Ezek. 38, Zech. 14 etc.) will bring equal devastation. To this the following responses are offered:

   (1) It appears that the invasion from the north will reduce Israel to such a state that they will actually be pleased to see the One they crucified saying, "Blessed is he that cometh in the name of the Lord" (Matt. 23:39). But unlike their experience at the hands of the Romans in AD 70, from this abject state they will be rescued, the Gentile invader destroyed, and Zion will be comforted and will recognise her King (Jer. 30:7,8; Isa. 40:1,2).

   (2) There is another way of looking at the statement "there shall be a time of trouble such as never was" etc. This form of expression appears to be a scriptural idiom seeking to convey the greatness of an event. E.g. "The locusts... [were] very grievous... before them were no such locusts as they, neither after them shall be such" (Exod. 10:14). Again, "A great people and a strong; there hath not been ever the like, neither shall be any more after it, even to the years of many generations" (Joel 2:2). (On this see T. Newton, *Dissertations on the Prophecies*, page 348.)

2. John Marshall makes an interesting comment on this — "What followed was, as Jesus said, tribulation such as was not since the beginning of the world to this time, no, nor ever shall be (Matt. 24:21), for a nation, a priesthood, a temple and holy city were all wiped out. In spite of judgement on Israel still to come, it will not be a complete destruction like that." (*CIL Bible Study Notes*, August 1972.)

3. Josephus, *Wars*, 5:10.5.

Concerning this great tribulation, Luke adds, "And they shall fall by the edge of the sword, and shall be led away captive into all nations" (21:24). This was a reiteration of the great prophecy that Moses uttered, even before Israel had entered the land:

> "And the LORD shall scatter thee among all people, from the one end of the earth even unto the other; and there thou shalt serve other gods, which neither thou nor thy fathers have known, even wood and stone." (Deut. 28:64)

And so it came to pass. Josephus reckoned that the number of the slain in the war was in excess of one million; whilst some hundred thousand were taken into captivity. From that day forwards, the Jews have been scattered throughout the world, testifying to the truth of these words of Jesus.

But this is not to continue for ever. Jesus continued, "And Jerusalem shall be trodden down of the Gentiles, **until** the times of the Gentiles be fulfilled" (Luke 21:24). So often, the re-establishment of the State of Israel in 1948 is declared to be the fulfilment of this verse. But a careful examination of Jesus' words will demonstrate that this cannot be so.

The key word is the word "until". "Jerusalem shall be trodden down of the Gentiles, **until** the times of the Gentiles be fulfilled" (v. 24). This means that when the times of the Gentiles are fulfilled, Jerusalem will no longer be trodden down of the Gentiles. What, then, are 'the times of the Gentiles'? [4] Have they been fulfilled?

---

4. Many refer this simply to the period of time that the Gentiles have exercised dominion over Israel. But, as Godet observes, "Would it not be a tautology to say: Jerusalem shall be trodden down by the Gentiles until the time of Gentile dominion comes to an end? Then the plural *kairoí*, the times, is not sufficiently accounted for on this view. Neither is the choice of the term *kairós*, the opportunity, instead of *chrónos*, a certain space of time. In Luke 19:44 the time *(kairós)* of Israel, denotes the season when God visits this people with the offer of salvation. According to this analogy, *the times of the Gentiles*, should designate the whole period during which God shall approach with His grace the Gentiles who have been hitherto strangers to His kingdom." (F. Godet, *The Gospel of St. Luke*, vol. 2, page 267.)

The word translated "times" is the Greek word *kairós*, which actually means 'season or opportunity'.[5] If "the times of the Gentiles" referred to a particular **period of time**, then the Greek word *chrónos* would have been more appropriate.[4] The "times of the Gentiles" thus refers to that period during which the **opportunity of salvation** is offered to the Gentiles — the **season** of Gentile opportunity.

Have "the times of the Gentiles" therefore been fulfilled? If they had, then there would be little point in preaching to the Gentiles and no Gentiles would be heeding the gospel call. Furthermore, consider what the Apostle Paul says of this matter: "Blindness in part is happened to Israel, **until** the fulness[6] of the Gentiles be come in" (Rom. 11:25). Again, notice the important word **"until"**. This means that when "the fulness of the Gentiles be come in" — or, in the words of Jesus, when "the times of the Gentiles be fulfilled" — **Israel will no longer be blind**. At that time, the words of Paul will be fulfilled:

> "And so all Israel shall be saved: as it is written, There shall come out of Sion the Deliverer, and shall turn away ungodliness from Jacob." (Rom. 11:26)

Israel today is still blind, and ignorant of the way of salvation, and will remain blind **until** the Deliverer comes out of Zion — a reference to the Lord Jesus Christ, who is to return to the earth as Israel's Deliverer. This means that the times of the Gentiles have

---

5. *Kairós* is translated "opportunity" on two occasions both of which illustrate its meaning: (1) "As we have therefore opportunity *(kairós)*, let us do good unto all men…" (Gal. 6:10). (2) "If they had been mindful of that country from whence they came out, they might have had opportunity *(kairós)* to have returned" (Heb. 11:15).

6. "Fulness", Gk. *plērōma*, denotes "that which has been completed, complement, plenitude, fullness." (G. Abbott-Smith, *Manual Greek Lexicon of the New Testament*, page 366). It thus here refers to the full number of Gentiles who are called and accept the gospel.

not yet been fulfilled. It is therefore wrong to interpret Luke 21:24 as referring to the establishment of the State of Israel in 1948.[7]

Furthermore, the prophets teach that there is to be a further treading down of Jerusalem by the Gentiles, this time at the hands of the Russian–Gog and his allies (Ezek. 38). Zechariah speaks of this future desolation:

> "Behold, the day of the LORD cometh, and thy spoil shall be divided in the midst of thee. For I will gather all nations against Jerusalem to battle; **and the city shall be taken,** and the houses rifled, and the women ravished; and half of the city shall go forth into captivity, and the residue of the people shall not be cut off from the city." (Zech. 14:1,2)

It is plain that the invasion of the Land of Israel at the time of the end is initially to be a **successful** invasion. For one brief period, the northern power will realise its aims, and will dominate the Middle East, and from thence the world, before being humiliated by the Lord. Daniel says, "And he (the invader from the north) shall plant the tabernacles of his palace between the seas in the glorious holy mountain; yet he shall come to his end, and none shall help him" (Dan. 11:45).

We are, then, still in the period of Jerusalem's downtreading, which commenced in AD 70, when the nation of Israel was overturned, and its inhabitants suffered "great tribulation, such as was not since the beginning of the world, nor ever shall be".

The Days Shortened

This time of tribulation was to be so severe that Jesus said, "Except those days should be shortened, there should no flesh be saved: but for the elect's sake those days shall be shortened"

---

7. This should not be seen as denying the significance of the regathering of the Jews, the establishment of the State of Israel and the liberation of Jerusalem which has taken place in the 19th and 20th centuries. Rather is it a more accurate perception of the significance of these events. If, as the prophets teach (Ezek. 38; Zech. 14 etc.), Israel is to be invaded by a Gentile power from the north then clearly there has to be an Israel in existence at the time of the end in order for that invasion to take place. This is the significance of what we now see in the land of Israel.

(Matt. 24:22). The siege proper commenced in April AD 70. By 26th September the whole city was in Titus' hands. In the Old Testament period it took Nebuchadnezzar king of Babylon almost 18 months to take Jerusalem (Jer. 52:4–7); it took Titus less than six months. Thus, although the siege was terrible in the extreme, it was relatively short. A number of factors combined to produce this shortening of the siege amongst which the following, already noted in passing on page 42, are perhaps the most important:

1. The number of Jews in the city was greatly swollen by those who, in spite of the Roman presence in the Holy Land, had flocked to Jerusalem to observe the Passover feast. This meant more mouths to feed.

2. The terrible civil war between the three opposing factions of the Jews within the city resulted in the destruction of a large part of the stored provisions. The historian notes:

   "Almost all the corn was burnt, which would have been sufficient for a siege of many years. So they were taken by the means of famine, which it was impossible they should have been, unless they had thus prepared the way for it by this procedure." [8]

Some of Israel's Flesh Saved

This shortening of the days of the siege resulted in the saving alive of some of Israel's flesh. This is also the theme of Joel 2:28–32, which cannot now be expounded in detail. We note simply at this point:

1. Joel 2:28 — "It shall come to pass afterward, that I will pour out my spirit upon all flesh; and your sons and your daughters shall prophesy, your old men shall dream dreams, your young men shall see visions." — This speaks of the pouring out of the Spirit on the day of Pentecost as stated by the apostle in Acts 2:16.

2. Joel 2:30–31 — "And I will shew wonders in the heavens and in the earth, blood, and fire, and pillars of smoke. The sun

---

8. Josephus, *Wars*, 5:1.4.

shall be turned into darkness, and the moon into blood, before the great and the terrible day of the LORD come." — This predicts the destruction of the nation of Israel consisting of its ruling heavens, and its ruled earth, which happened in AD 70 — more on this in Chapter 7.

3. Joel 2:32—"And it shall come to pass, that **whosoever** shall call on the name of the LORD shall be delivered." — Paul testifies in Romans 10:13, that this has reference to the bringing in of the Gentiles that took place in the years leading up to the destruction of Jerusalem.

4. The point we wish to emphasise occurs in the second part of verse 32 which says, "In mount Zion and in Jerusalem there shall be **those that escape**" (RV). This is the same teaching as Matthew 24:22, that some of Israel's flesh would be saved.

Jesus said that the days would be shortened and some of Israel's flesh saved "for the elect's sake". Who, then, are "the elect"? The following scriptures would suggest that they are the believers:

> "And shall not God avenge his own elect?" (These are the believers who suffered at the hands of the Jews in the period leading up to the "days of vengeance" upon Israel.) (Luke 18:7)
>
> "Put on therefore, as the elect of God, holy and beloved, bowels of mercies, kindness, humbleness of mind, meekness, longsuffering." (Col. 3:12)
>
> "Peter, an apostle of Jesus Christ, to the elect who are sojourners of the Dispersion in Pontus, Galatia, Cappadocia, Asia, and Bithynia." (1 Peter 1:1 RV)

For the believers' sakes, then, the days of tribulation were shortened and some of Israel's flesh were saved, and are with us today as the Jewish people. If Israel's flesh had ceased to exist, then God's promises concerning them could not have been fulfilled. They are the people of the "great nation" promised to Abraham (Gen. 12:2) over which the apostles will have jurisdiction (Matt. 19:28). From that nation the laws of God will go out to illuminate the darkness of the Gentile world (Isa. 2:3). They are to be the people that will form the nucleus of God's future Kingdom (Mic. 4:6–8). The establishment of this kingdom is that for which the elect all down the ages have longed and prayed. So for the elect's sake God preserved the Jews, working with them throughout subsequent history to fulfil his promises. Even Titus, the leader of the Roman armies, acknowledged the hand of God in bringing events to a swift conclusion, for he is reported as saying:

> "We have certainly had God for our assistant in this war, and it was no other than God who ejected the Jews out of these fortifications, for what could the hands of men, or any machines, do toward overthrowing these towers?" [9]

A coin of the Roman Emperor Vespasian issued to commemorate the fall of Jerusalem in AD 70. It shows a Jewish woman under a palm tree with a Roman soldier standing by. It carries the words *JUDAEA CAPTA* — Judaea conquered

9. Josephus, *Wars*, 6:9.1.

CHAPTER SIX

THE CARCASE AND THE EAGLES

Matthew 24

23 Then if any man shall say unto you, Lo, here is Christ, or there; believe it not. 24 For there shall arise false Christs, and false prophets, and shall shew great signs and wonders; insomuch that, if it were possible, they shall deceive the very elect. 25 Behold, I have told you before. 26 Wherefore if they shall say unto you, Behold, he is in the desert; go not forth: behold, he is in the secret chambers; believe it not. 27 For as the lightning cometh out of the east, and shineth even unto the west; so shall also the coming of the Son of man be. 28 For wheresoever the carcase is, there will the eagles be gathered together.

Mark 13

21 And then if any man shall say to you, Lo, here is Christ; or, lo, he is there; believe him not: 22 For false Christs and false prophets shall rise, and shall shew signs and wonders, to seduce, if it were possible, even the elect. 23 But take ye heed: behold, I have foretold you all things.

Luke 21

There can be no doubt that this section, Matthew 24:23–28, is a parenthesis. Verse 21 speaks of the "great tribulation" that was to take place in those days and verse 29 continues to speak of "the tribulation **of those days**". Verses 23–28, which appear between the two tribulation verses, have to do with things that were to take place in those days of tribulation. The verses may be set out diagrammatically:

VERSE 21 — **"Then shall be great tribulation..."**

↓ **(Verses 23–28)**

VERSE 29 — **"Immediately after the tribulation of those days..."**

In this parenthesis the Lord communicated to his disciples a most important message. It would be a time of false messiahs and false hopes. Men would come bringing tidings of miracle-workers in the desert – we have earlier referred to examples on pages 19-21. As the crisis of AD 70 approached, the situation would become worse. Even the elect would be in danger of being deceived. The advice of Jesus must remain in their minds – "Go not forth... believe it not" (v. 26).

When the coming of Jesus of which they had enquired arrived, there would be no mistake – "For as the lightning cometh out of the east, and shineth even unto the west; so shall also the coming of the Son of man be. For wheresoever the carcase is, there will the eagles be gathered together."

They had asked, "What shall be the sign of thy coming?" (Matt. 24:3). The word here translated "coming" occurs nowhere else in the gospels except in this one chapter. It is the Greek word *parousía,* which does not mean appearing, manifestation or revealing. It means simply 'presence'. *Parousía,* presence, may refer to either a visible or an invisible presence.[1] It has reference

---

1. "*Parousía* (παρουσία), literally, 'a presence', [derived from] *para,* 'with', and *ousia,* 'being' (from *eimi,* 'to be')." (W. E. Vine, *Expository Dictionary of New Testament Words*, vol. 1, page 208). The word itself does not denote either a visible or invisible presence. Clearly when Paul wrote, "I am glad of the coming (*parousía*) of Stephanas and Fortunatus and Achaicus: for that which was lacking on your part they have supplied" (1 Cor. 16:17), a visible presence was being referred to. But it is also evident that when he wrote to the Corinthians, "For I verily, as absent in body, but present (*páreimi*, the verbal form of *parousía*) in spirit, have judged already, as though I were present, concerning him that hath so done this deed" (1 Cor. 5:3) he was speaking of an invisible presence.

The use of the word by Josephus, who wrote in Greek and was contemporary with the apostles, supports the view that *parousía* means presence, not the act of coming, and that it may be used of an ***invisible*** presence. Speaking of the cloud which appeared when the angel took up residence in the tabernacle he writes: "There was a mist over the tabernacle... from it there dropped a sweet dew, and such a one as showed the presence *(parousía)* of God to those that desired and believed it" (*Antiquities*, 3:8.5). Of the invisible angelic presence at Dothan in the time of Elisha (2 Kings 6:15–18) he writes: "[Elisha] besought God to make manifest to his servant his power and presence *(parousía)*, so far as was

[Footnote continued on next page]

here to the Lord's invisible presence in Israel in AD 70 for the purpose of judging the nation, and not to his second appearing for which we are still looking.[2]

It is interesting to ask why Matthew alone should use this particular word when recounting the disciples' question. It is very unlikely that the conversation took place in Greek for Jesus and his disciples spoke Aramaic (e.g. Mark 5:41; 7:34 where Aramaic words that Jesus used are transliterated). By New Testament times the word *parousía* had acquired a technical meaning, being used of royal and imperial visits to a city or province.[3] These state visits were frequently marked by the minting of special coins[4] and medals. Matthew, the tax collector, was no doubt very familiar with such coins and knew about this technical meaning of *parousía*. *Parousía* would be an ideal word to express the idea of Jesus visiting the land of Israel for the purpose of judgement.

When the Lord came in judgement against Israel there would be no mistake. It would be, to the faithful observers of the signs of the times, like the "lightning [coming] out of the east and

---

possible, in order to the inspiring of him with hope and courage" (*Antiquities*, 9:4.3).

2. John Thomas so understood the meaning of *parousía* in the passage before us. He comments, "Immediately after the tribulation of those days shall the sun be darkened and the moon shall not give her light, and the stars shall fall from heaven… These were the lights in which there were to be 'great signs and fearful sights,' indicative of the παρουσία, or presence, ***though invisible***, of the Son of Man when the Graeco–Roman army should be sent by him to destroy the city of his murderers." (*Eureka—An Exposition of the Apocalypse*, vol. 2, page 272.)

H. P. Mansfield comments: "To the discerning mind, educated in the Old Testament prophecies and the instruction of the Lord Jesus, the Roman attack on Jerusalem in AD 70 and the subsequent judgement were the tokens of the presence of Christ in power… The destruction of Jerusalem testified to the power and authority of the Lord Jesus, as well as his presence supervising the judgement." (*Guidebook to the Gospels*, page 110.)

3. G. Friedrich and G. Kittel, *Theological Dictionary of the New Testament*, vol. 5, page 860. G. A. Deissmann, *Light From the Ancient East*, page 368.

4. E.g. that produced in Corinth on the coming of Nero (G. Friedrich and G. Kittel, *Theological Dictionary of the New Testament*, page 860).

[shining] even to the west" (v. 27).[5] There would not be any doubt at all, for they would see "the eagles" coming to prey upon "the carcase" (v. 28), and would thus know that the Lord was present for judgement.[6]

By using these words Jesus was directing them to Deuteronomy ch. 28:

> "The LORD shall cause thee to be smitten before thine enemies: thou shalt go out one way against them, and flee seven ways before them: and shalt be removed into all the kingdoms of the earth. And **thy carcase** shall be meat unto all **fowls of the air**, and unto the beasts of the earth, and no man shall fray them away... The LORD shall bring a nation against thee from far, from the end of the earth, **as swift as the eagle flieth;** a nation whose tongue thou shalt not understand... And he shall besiege thee in all thy gates, until thy high and fenced walls come down, wherein thou trustedst, throughout all thy land: and he shall besiege thee in all thy gates throughout all thy land, which the LORD thy God hath given thee." (Deut. 28:25,26,49,52)

It is interesting to note that Jeremiah referred to this scripture with reference to the Babylonian invasion:

---

5. "The word ***lightning*** (Greek *astrapē*) occurs 9 times in the New Testament. In Luke 11:36 it is rendered as *'bright shining'*, that is, '*as when the bright shining of a candle doth give thee light'*. In other places, e.g. Rev. 4:5; 8:5 etc., it is associated with thunderstorms. The word comes from the root *astraptō*, which in Luke 24:4 refers to the shining garments of the two angels at the sepulchre. The use of the word in Matt. 24:27 may probably be understood in the more general sense of the light shining out of the east as the dawn appears and eventually spreading even unto the west." (J. Knowles, *The Olivet Prophecy*, page 25.)

Thus in the words "as the lightning cometh out of the east, and shineth even unto the west" may be conveyed the idea that the judgements of God were to pass over the land like the searching light of the sun, which rises in the east and sets in the west, systematically seeking out all the hidden things of darkness. This idea is in fact supported by the words that follow — "***Wheresoever*** the carcase is ..."— not only in Jerusalem.

6. John Thomas commented as follows on the sense of Jesus' words: "But my apostles, or disciples, 'When they shall say unto YOU [not to persons of the 19th Century] Behold he is in the desert [of Judea] — go not forth; Behold he is in the secret chambers, believe it not,' for he shall not come privately. 'For as the lightening cometh out of the east, and shineth even unto the west; so [publicly] shall the coming of the Son of man be.' 'FOR' this is the manner of his coming; 'Wheresoever the carcase is, there will the eagles be gathered together'." ("The Mount Olivet Prophecy", *Herald of the Kingdom and Age to Come*, vol. 10, page 257.)

> "And the **carcases** of this people shall be meat for the **fowls of the heaven,** and for the beasts of the earth; and none shall fray them away. Then will I cause to cease from the cities of Judah, and from the streets of Jerusalem, the voice of mirth, and the voice of gladness, the voice of the bridegroom, and the voice of the bride: for the land shall be desolate." (Jer. 7:33–34).

> "And I will make void the counsel of Judah and Jerusalem in this place; and I will cause them to fall by the sword before their enemies, and by the hands of them that seek their lives: and **their carcases** will I give to be meat for the **fowls of the heaven,** and for the beasts of the earth." (Jer. 19:7)

The first of these references from Jeremiah is of more than passing interest since Jesus quoted from Jeremiah 7:11 on the day before the Olivet Prophecy was given (Matt. 21:13). The following table shows some of the parallels between Jeremiah ch. 7 and the words that Jesus spoke around the time the Olivet Prophecy was given:

JEREMIAH 7	MATTHEW 21–24
"Stand in the gate of the ***LORD's house***..." (v.2)	"Jesus went into *the temple*..." (21:12).
"Is this house ...become *a den of robbers* in your eyes?" (v.11)	"My house... ye have made it ***a den of thieves***" (21:13)
"Mine anger... shall be poured out... it shall ***burn***, and shall not be quenched" (v.20)	"He sent forth his armies... and ***burned*** up their city" (22:7).
"The LORD hath rejected and forsaken ***the generation*** of his wrath" (v.29)	"Ye generation of vipers... ***This generation*** shall not pass, till all these things be fulfilled" (23:33; 24:34)
"The days come... it shall no more be called... ***the valley of the son of Hinnom***, but the valley of slaughter ..." (v.32)	"How can ye escape the damnation of *hell*? (Gk. *gehenna* = '***valley of Hinnom***')" (23:33)
"The ***carcases*** of this people shall be meat for the ***fowls of the heaven***" (v.33)	"Wheresoever the ***carcase*** is, there will ***the eagles*** be gathered together" (24:28)

Thus Jesus, like Jeremiah, was pronouncing impending judgement on this wicked nation that had now filled up the cup of its iniquity. The carcase was the body politic of Israel (Deut. 28:25,26). The eagle was the power of Rome — the nation of fierce countenance from afar (Deut. 28:49,50). The Roman eagle descending viciously on the Israel–carcase was to be the sign to the faithful that the Lord had come in judgement and that the Mosaic age had finally reached its end.

The eagle standard of Rome

CHAPTER SEVEN

SUN, MOON AND STARS

Matthew 24

29 Immediately after the
tribulation of those days
shall the sun be darkened,
and the moon shall not give
her light, and the stars shall
fall from heaven, and the
powers of the heavens shall
be shaken: 30 And then
shall appear the sign of the
Son of man in heaven: and
then shall all the tribes of
the earth mourn, and they
shall see the Son of man
coming in the clouds of
heaven with power and
great glory. 31 And he shall
send his angels with a great
sound of a trumpet, and
they shall gather together
his elect from the four
winds, from one end of
heaven to the other.

Mark 13

24 But in those days, after
that tribulation, the sun shall
be darkened, and the moon
shall not give her light,
25 And the stars of heaven
shall fall, and the powers
that are in heaven shall be
shaken. 26 And then shall
they see the Son of man
coming in the clouds with
great power and glory.
27 And then shall he send
his angels, and shall gather
together his elect from the
four winds, from the
uttermost part of the earth
to the uttermost part of
heaven.

Luke 21

25 And there shall be signs
in the sun, and in the moon,
and in the stars; and upon
the earth distress of
nations, with perplexity; the
sea and the waves roaring;
26 Men's hearts failing them
for fear, and for looking
after those things which are
coming on the earth: for the
powers of heaven shall be
shaken. 27 And then shall
they see the Son of man
coming in a cloud with
power and great glory.
28 And when these things
begin to come to pass, then
look up, and lift up your
heads; for your redemption
draweth nigh.

Context

At this point it will be as well to remind ourselves of the way in which the context links the events in the sun, moon and stars with the AD 70 period. This may perhaps best be seen in the Mark record. Having spoken of the "abomination of desolation... standing where it ought not" Jesus then told his disciples that would be the time for those "in Judaea [to] flee to the mountains" (Mark 13:14). He then made the following statements in connection with this time of emergency:

1. "Woe to them that are with child... **in those days**" (v. 17).
2. "**In those days** shall be affliction ('tribulation' RV), such as was not from the beginning of the creation..."(v.19).
3. "Except that the Lord had shortened **those days**, no flesh should be saved" (v.20).

4. "**In those days**, after that tribulation, the sun shall be darkened, and the moon shall not give her light, And the stars of heaven shall fall, and the powers that are in heaven shall be shaken" (vv. 24–25).

The connection of the events in the sun, moon and stars with the events of **"those days"** is undeniable. The Matthew record reinforces this.

Immediately

Matthew 24:29 begins, "Immediately after the tribulation of those days shall the sun be darkened…" Whatever might be involved in the verses that follow—whatever events are being described by the darkening of the sun, moon and stars, the shaking of the powers of the heavens and the appearing of the Son of man in heaven—of one thing we can be certain: all these things were to take place "**immediately** after the tribulation".

The Greek word translated "immediately" (Gk. *eutheōs*[1]) conveys exactly the same idea as the English word, and by no stretch of imagination can it be made to signify 2,000 years hence! The same word is found in the following verses where the meaning of the word is very clear:

> "And Jesus put forth his hand, and touched him, saying, I will; be thou clean. And **immediately** (Gk. *eutheōs*) his leprosy was cleansed." (Matt. 8:3)
>
> "And **immediately** (Gk. *eutheōs*) Jesus stretched forth his hand, and caught him, and said unto him, O thou of little faith, wherefore didst thou doubt?" (Matt. 14:31)
>
> "So Jesus had compassion on them, and touched their eyes: and **immediately** (Gk. *eutheōs*) their eyes received sight, and they followed him." (Matt. 20:34)

[1] "εὐθέως, straightway, at once, directly" (G. Abbott-Smith, *Manual Greek Lexicon of the New Testament*, page 186). "*Eutheōs*, εὐθέως, at once, straightway" (W. E. Vine, *Expository Dictionary of New Testament Words*, vol. 2, page 127). "εὐθέως, *euthéōs*; adv. from *euthús*, straight, immediate. Immediately, instantly, straightway, forthwith… By implication meaning shortly" (S. Zodhiates, *The Complete Word Study Dictionary: New Testament*, page 673).

In each case it is seen that *euthēos* means 'straightway', 'immediately'. This is such an obvious point that it might almost seem superfluous to make it; but it is precisely at this point in the Olivet Prophecy that many expositors make their jump from AD 70 to the present day.[2] This is especially the case with Luke ch. 21, where the word "immediately" does not occur. The parallel record in Luke reads thus: "And Jerusalem shall be trodden down of the Gentiles, until the times of the Gentiles be fulfilled. And there shall be signs in the sun, and in the moon, and in the stars"(vv. 24, 25). It is common practice to interpret the "signs in the sun, and in the moon, and in the stars", and everything that follows, as referring to the end of the times of the Gentiles.[3] This, however, cannot be. The presence of the word "immediately" in the Matthew 24:29 record indicates that the signs in the sun, moon and stars would follow directly after "the tribulation of those days".[4]

---

2. The following is an example: "The word ***immediately*** would seem to link [Jesus'] comments with them that precede them, and which relate to the overthrow of AD 70, but the word can be rendered ***suddenly***, and perhaps relates to the suddenness by which current events will develop at the time of the end." (H. P. Mansfield, *Guidebook to the Gospels*, page 110.)

This is not the case. *Euthēos* occurs 80 times in the New Testament and is never translated "suddenly". It does not mean "suddenly". It means "immediately". The explanation advanced in the above quotation is an attempt to evade the obvious — the signs in the sun, moon and stars were to be expected immediately after the tribulation of those days.

3. E.g. "The sun, moon and stars in this portion of [the Olivet Prophecy] relate to the Gentiles." (H. P. Mansfield, *Guidebook to the Gospels*, page 110.)

4. John Thomas correctly comments: "In the glowing imagery of prophecy... "the sun" of Israel was eclipsed, or "darkened," its moon no longer gave its light, its stars fell from heaven, and the powers of its heaven were shaken. Such was the fact; for the executive and Aaronic and Levitical hierarchy were abolished, and the nobles of Israel fell from their high estate, and the subordinate powers of the state were shaken... All this happened ***immediately*** after the tribulation of the siege..." ("The Prophecy of Mount Olivet", *Herald of the Kingdom and Age to Come*, vol. 10, page 275.)

THE LORD'S MOUNT OLIVET PROPHECY

There is described by Jesus an unbroken chain of events that links Matthew 24:29 with the events of AD 70, which may be summarised diagrammatically thus:

> 1 ↓
>
> **ABOMINATION OF DESOLATION**
> **standing in the holy place... (v. 15)**
> **(The Roman invasion)**
>
> 2 ↓
>
> **THEN**
> **shall be great tribulation... (v. 21)**
> **(The siege of Jerusalem)**
>
> 3
>
> **IMMEDIATELY AFTER**
> **the tribulation of those days shall the sun be darkened... (v. 29)**
> **(Effects of the siege)**

Before examining in turn the events that were to follow immediately upon the great tribulation, we must note the sequence of events described:

1. There would be signs in the heavens—the sun would be darkened, the moon would not give light and the stars would fall from heaven; the powers of the heaven would be shaken (Matt. 24:29; Mark 13:24,25; Luke 21:25).
2. There would be signs on the earth, distress of nations with perplexity; the sea and the waves roaring; men's hearts failing them for fear (Luke 21:25,26).
3. The sign that the Son of man was in heaven would be seen (Matt. 24:30). It is important to note that this is the sense of the words—not that there would be seen some mysterious sign in the heavens.[5]

---

5. Some writers direct attention to the fact that Josephus, *Wars*, 6:5.3, describes a number of allegedly literal portents appearing in the heavens just prior to the fall of Jerusalem. But his views on "signs" were very much influenced by the pagan view of things — e.g. just prior to the death of Herod Agrippa the First

4. The tribes of the earth would then mourn and (note this carefully) **they** would see the Son of man coming in the clouds of heaven with power and great glory (Matt. 24:30; Mark 13:26; Luke 21:27).
5. Jesus would send his angels with the great sound of a trumpet to gather the elect from the four winds (Matt. 24:31; Mark 13:27).
6. The beginning of the fulfilment of these things would indicate that the disciples' redemption was drawing nigh (Luke 21:28).

These were the events which Jesus said would **immediately** follow the tribulation **of those days** and which we must now consider.

1. Signs in sun, moon and stars

The language that Jesus uses here is taken from the Old Testament prophets. In the world of nature, the heavens rule over the earth. So we read that "God made two great lights; the greater light **to rule** the day, the lesser light **to rule** the night" (Gen. 1:16; see also Psalm 136:8–9). Thus seed-time and harvest, summer and winter, day and night are all controlled by the relationship of the heavenly bodies to the earth over which they "rule". (Recent scientific discoveries are beginning to reveal the extent to which they exert their influence.) The prophetic scriptures take hold of this relationship of heavenly bodies to the earth and apply it to the political world. The mass of humanity in a kingdom is styled "the earth", and the rulers who are exalted over the people are described as "the heavens". "Heavens" in the Hebrew is *sāmayim* (pronounced *shamayim*), from a root that means 'to be high'.[6] Thus

---

[Scripture record Acts 12:23] Josephus records (*Antiquities*, 19:8.2): "As [Herod] looked up he saw an owl sitting on a certain rope over his head, and immediately understood that this bird was the messenger of ill tidings..." It was ***not*** to this type of augury that Jesus referred.

6. J. McClintock and J. Strong, *Cyclopaedia of Biblical, Theological and Ecclesiastical Literature*, vol. 4, page 123: "*shama'yim,* [is] the plural of an obsolete noun... the idea expressed by the word is *height, elevation.*"

the heavens, which are "high above the earth", constitute a fitting symbol of those men elevated above the mass of humanity as rulers. This way of speaking about a nation is used in the prophetic scriptures especially with reference to the nation of Israel. The following are examples:

DEUTERONOMY 32: In this chapter, Jehovah is addressing the nation of Israel and he begins by saying, "Give ear, O ye **heavens,** and I will speak; and hear, O **earth**, the words of my mouth" (v.1). He tells them of his ultimate purpose and how that in the outworking of this he has chosen Israel to be his own special people – "The LORD'S portion is his people; Jacob is the lot of his inheritance" (v.9). At v.15, speaking of things that are not as though they are, he predicts the way in which Israel will forget God and lightly esteem the Rock of his salvation. Because of this rejection of God's grace (which culminated in them crucifying their Saviour) God will reject them and turn to the Gentiles – "I will move them to jealousy with those which are not a people; I will provoke them to anger with a foolish nation" (v.21, and see Rom. 10:19 where this is quoted and applied by Paul to the bringing in of the Gentiles). God, having turned to the Gentiles, will then judge his people as depicted in v.22 – "For a fire is kindled in mine anger, and shall burn unto the lowest hell, and shall **consume the earth** with her increase…"

Thus in this chapter we have reference to Israel as consisting of "heavens" and "earth", and, although the destruction of the heavens is not mentioned, there is reference to the AD 70 burning up of the earth – an aspect of the subject which is considered in greater detail elsewhere, e.g. 2 Peter ch. 3 (see pages 70–73).

PSALM 102: The nation of Israel, politically organised under the Mosaic Law Covenant, was created by God through the mediation of angels at Sinai (Acts 7:53; Gal. 3:19). It was there that He gave to them the law and entered into covenant with them. It is this creation of Israel with its heavens and earth that is referred to in Psalm 102:25–26:

"Of old hast thou laid the foundation of **the earth;** and **the heavens** are the work of thy hands. They shall perish, but thou shalt endure: yea, all of them shall wax old like a garment; as a vesture shalt thou change them, and they shall be changed."

That this creation of heavens and earth, their subsequent waxing old and changing, refers to the nation of Israel is seen by the way in which the Psalm is taken up in the letter to the Hebrews. There the writer seeks, by the spirit, to demonstrate that Christ is "better than" the angels, and contrasts the kingdom established by angels at Sinai with the kingdom of the Son of God. The throne of the Son of God is to be "for ever and ever", but the heavens and earth of which the Psalmist spoke are to "perish"; "wax old as doth a garment"; "be changed" (Heb. 1:11,12). This reference to Israel under the Mosaic arrangement as heavens and earth that would "wax old" is taken up later by the apostle in a way that confirms this exposition. In chapter 8 he contrasts the new covenant in Christ with the old covenant arrangement established by the angels, and he says, "In that he saith, A new covenant, he hath made the first old. Now that which decayeth and **waxeth old** is ready to vanish away" (Heb. 8:13). When this letter to the Hebrews was written, the time had almost arrived when, as a result of the Roman invasion, the Mosaic system was to be destroyed.[7]

ISAIAH 51: Isaiah, on a number of occasions, speaks of Israel as consisting of heavens and earth, but none is more relevant to the Olivet Prophecy than chapter 51. Verse 5 of this chapter speaks of God's saving work on behalf of His people — "My salvation is gone forth". However, Israel will reject it and God will turn to the Gentiles — "The isles shall wait upon me, and on mine arm shall they trust". But what about the nation of Israel? — "Lift up your eyes to the **heavens**, and look upon the **earth** beneath: for the heavens shall vanish away like smoke, and the earth shall wax old like a garment, and they that dwell therein shall die in like manner…" (v.6). Thus Israel will be destroyed as a nation, and the

---

[7] For a more detailed consideration of the use of Psalm 102:25 in Hebrews ch. 1, see J. Allfree, *Trinitarian Texts Examined*, page 38.

reason is given (with clear reference to Deuteronomy 32:15)—"[thou] forgettest the LORD thy maker, that hath stretched forth the heavens, and laid the foundations of the earth" (v.13). This is the same creation of heavens and earth to which Psalm 102 refers, i.e. the creation of Israel at Sinai; and that it is this creation of Israel that is referred to under the figure of the making of heavens and earth is abundantly clear from v.16. There the prophet proceeds to speak of the future restoration of Israel using the same figure — "I have covered thee in the shadow of mine hand, that I may plant the **heavens,** and lay the foundations of **the earth,** and say **unto Zion,** Thou art my people."

Thus far we have been considering the way in which the prophetic scriptures speak of Israel as heavens and earth, and we are thus helped to understand the words of Jesus when he says, "Heaven and earth shall pass away, but my words shall not pass away" (Matt. 24:35). We must now proceed to consider specifically the constituent parts of the heavens, which are mentioned by Jesus — the sun, moon and stars.

DANIEL 8: This chapter describes the vision of the ram and the he-goat to which we have before referred (page 37). The goat represents the power of Greece, and the notable horn between its eyes represents Alexander the Great. This horn was to be broken, and "four notable ones" would arise in its place, which foretold the division of Alexander's empire into four by his generals Cassander, Lysimachus, Ptolemy and Seleucus. Upon the territory of one of these would emerge the "little horn" power which history subsequently revealed to be the power of Rome. Rome appeared as a power in the East, on the Seleucid division of Alexander's empire, when it conquered Syria in BC 65. This little horn power had a work "before ordained of God" against the nation of Israel. He would conquer Israel ("the pleasant land"—v.9); would be the instrument whereby Israel's prince would be put to death; would take away the daily sacrifice and would destroy the Temple (v.11). This work of the little horn in judging God's people is further spoken of in verse 10 where we are told that he "waxed great, even to the host of **heaven**: and it cast down some of the host and of **the stars** to the ground, and stamped upon them". Here, then, the 'leading lights' in Israel are spoken of as "the stars of heaven."

JOEL 2: There can be no doubt that verse 28 of this chapter was fulfilled on that first Pentecost after the ascension of Jesus, as recorded in Acts ch. 2, when the holy spirit was poured out on the believers. Peter, referring to this pouring out of the holy spirit said, "This is that[8] which was spoken by the prophet Joel; and it shall come to pass in the **last days**, saith God, I will pour out of my Spirit upon all flesh..." (Joel 2:28; Acts 2:16, 17).

Note, first of all, that Peter said that the things of which Joel prophesied were **then** taking place, and that those days were **"the last days"**. Paul confirmed that they were the "last days" when, writing to the Hebrews, he said, "God hath in **these last days** spoken unto us by his Son" (Heb. 1:2). They were the last days of the nation of Israel under the Mosaic arrangement.[9]

As already noted in chapter 5 (page 52) Joel speaks of three things that were to happen in those days:

1. The pouring out of the spirit — "I will pour out my spirit upon all flesh" (Joel 2:28,29).
2. The bringing in of the Gentiles — "It shall come to pass, that **whosoever** shall call on the name of the LORD shall be delivered" (Joel 2:32).
3. In those same "last days" there will be "wonders in the heavens and in the earth, blood, and fire, and pillars of smoke. The sun shall be turned into darkness, and the moon into blood, before the great and terrible day of the LORD come" (Joel 2:30, 31).

---

8. The force of these words of the apostle must be noted. He did not say, "This is something similar to that which Joel predicted." Neither was he mistaken as has been suggested. What was happening ***then*** was the fulfilment of Joel's words in the fullest sense.

9. See footnote 19, page 16, for further testimony on this.

Thus Joel, using the familiar figure of the nation of Israel consisting of heavens and earth, graphically speaks of the destruction of the nation that followed less than 40 years after the pouring out of the spirit on the believers on the day of Pentecost.

2 PETER 3: Since Peter quoted this passage from Joel on the day of Pentecost, it is of interest, and relevant to our study of the words of the Lord (for Peter was with him on the Mount of Olives), to see how he later refers again to this impending destruction of Israel's heavens and earth when he writes his second epistle to the Jewish brethren. It is a letter of warning of impending judgement. He seeks to remind them of things spoken "by the holy prophets" (such as those we have been considering) and "the apostles" (such as himself on the day of Pentecost) (v. 2). He tells them:

1. There will be scoffers **in the last days** (v. 3) — i.e. the same "last days" to which he referred in Acts 2:17 — the days which see the outpouring of the holy spirit and the subsequent offering of salvation to the Gentiles.
2. These scoffers will deny the "coming", i.e. the *parousía,* of the Lord Jesus (v. 4) — the very event about which he, with James, Andrew and John, enquired on the Mount of Olives, i.e. the coming of Jesus in judgement against Israel.
3. But the time of judgement **will** come, for "the heavens and the earth, which are now (i.e. when he wrote the letter)... are kept in store, reserved unto fire against the day of judgment and perdition of ungodly men" (v.7).
4. Meanwhile, the longsuffering of God waits for the erring Jewish brethren to mend their ways, but the time will come when "**the heavens** shall pass away with a great noise, and the elements melt with fervent heat, **the earth** also and the works that are therein shall be burned up" (v.10 and cf. Deut. 32:22). Peter adds here a new feature providing an interesting point of confirmation of the soundness of this exposition:

(a) He refers to the heavens passing away — Israel's high and official places, which passed away in AD 70, as mentioned by Moses, Joel, Isaiah, Paul and by Jesus in the Olivet Prophecy.

(b) He speaks of the burning up of the earth as mentioned elsewhere too, i.e. the destruction of the nation as a result of the Roman invasion.

(c) But he also refers to the **"elements"** melting with the heat of that day of judgement. It is Paul who explains what these "elements" are when he rebukes the Galatians for wanting to return to the Law — "how turn ye again to the weak and beggarly **elements**, whereunto ye desire again to be in bondage?" (Gal. 4:3,9).[10] The elements were the essential constituent parts of the Law without which it could not be kept. By destroying the temple, removing the priesthood, scattering the people, the elements were destroyed.

5. Thus Peter, using the language of the prophets and of his Lord, describes the destruction of Israel which happened in AD 70. But he then looks to the future, and taking up the theme of Isaiah 51:16 to which we have earlier referred, says, "We, according to his promise, look for **new heavens** and a **new earth**, wherein dwelleth righteousness" (v.13)[11] — the future restoration of Israel as God's kingdom.

---

10. The word "elements" is the Greek *stoicheíon*. W. E. Vine (*Expository Dictionary of New Testament Words*, vol. 2, page 22) writes, "STOICHEION (στοιχεῖον), used in the plural, primarily signifies any first things from which others in a series, or a composite whole, take their rise; the word denotes an element, first principle..."

In addition to the two occurrences in 2 Peter 3 and these in Galatians 4, it is found only in Colossians 2:8,20 (translated "rudiments") and in Hebrews 5:12 (translated, "first principles"). In both of these a careful examination of the context will show that, in these places also, the *stoicheíon* refer to the Law of Moses. See also footnote 1, page 112.

11. This appears to be a composite quotation. Firstly from Isaiah 65:17 — "I create new heavens and a new earth" — and then Isaiah 45:8, a prophecy of the

Thus we may conclude that, in Matthew 24:29, when Jesus speaks of the sun being darkened, the moon not giving her light and the stars falling from heaven, he is using the language of the prophets and is speaking of the political destruction of the nation of Israel.

2. The powers of the heavens shall be shaken

All three records of the Olivet Prophecy inform us that having spoken of the signs in the sun, moon and stars, Jesus adds, "And the powers of the heavens shall be shaken" (Matt. 24:29; Mark 13:25; Luke 21:26). Here we have confirmation, if it were needed, that the celestial upheavals of which the Lord has been speaking have to do with the dissolution of Israel's commonwealth as organised under the Law Covenant.

The apostle in his letter to the Hebrews used this same figure of speech. Earlier he has emphasised the temporary nature of the Law Covenant and made the point that even as he is writing the letter, "That which decayeth and waxeth old is ready to vanish away" (8:13). However, many of the Hebrew brethren were inclined to return to an observance of the Law as a means of salvation. For this reason the apostle writes to them in chapter 12: "Ye are not come unto the mount that might be touched… But ye are come unto mount Sion, and unto the city of the living God, the heavenly Jerusalem… And to Jesus the mediator of the new covenant…" (vv. 18–24). He goes on to exhort them to "refuse not him that speaketh… Whose voice (at the giving of the Law Covenant from Sinai) then shook the earth: but now (here he quotes Haggai 2:6) he hath promised, saying, Yet once more I shake not the earth only, but also heaven. And this word, Yet once more, signifieth the removing of those things that are shaken, as of things that are made, that those things which cannot be shaken may remain" (vv. 25–27). The Old Covenant arrangement had waxed old and was about to be removed. It was to be shaken out of existence by the impending events of AD 70. How foolish to

regeneration of Israel which speaks of "the heavens" pouring down righteousness upon "the earth" that responds by bringing forth salvation and letting "righteousness spring up".

want to return to it. The New Covenant arrangement "cannot be shaken." This would endure and its complete fulfilment realised in the establishment of the coming Kingdom.

3. Signs upon the earth (Luke 21:25,26)

Not only will there be signs in Israel's heavens; but there will also be signs "upon the earth" – that is, among the common people of the land. Jesus says:

> "And there shall be signs in sun and moon and stars; **and upon the earth** distress of nations, in perplexity for the roaring of the sea and the billows." (Luke 21:25 RV)

Since the sun, moon and stars refer to Israel's rulers, it follows, on the basis of scriptures already referred to, that "the earth" represents the people who are ruled over. That there is indeed to be distress upon the land of Israel is a point emphasised earlier by the Lord. He said, "Woe unto them that are with child and to them that give suck in those days! for there shall be great distress upon the earth, and wrath unto this people" (v. 23 RVm).

But if "the earth" refers to the inhabitants of the land of Israel, why does Jesus use the plural, saying, "And upon the earth distress of **nations**"? The Greek word translated "nations" is *éthnos,* and it usually refers to Gentiles when used in the plural, as it is here.[12]

A number of Gentile races had settled in the land of Israel and formed part of Israel's political "earth". J. Stuart Russell makes the following comment:

> "In our Lord's time it was usual to speak of the inhabitants of Palestine as consisting of several nations. Josephus speaks of 'the nation of the Samaritans', 'the nation of the Batanaeans', 'the nation of the Galileans'—using the very word *ethnos* (ἔθνος) which we find in the passage before us.

---

12. "ETHNOS, ἔθνος, originally a multitude, denotes *(a)* a nation or people… *(b)* in the plural, the nations as distinct from Israel." (W. E. Vine, *Expository Dictionary of New Testament Words*, vol. 3, page 102). The use of the word in Acts 2:5 with reference to Jews does not contradict this — they were Jews assembled in Jerusalem to keep the feast of Pentecost. They had come there "***out of*** every nation…"

> Judea was a distinct nation, often with a king of its own; so also Samaria, Batanea, Trachonitis, Itrurea, Abilene, — all of which had at different times princes with the title Ethnarch, a name which signifies the ruler of a nation." [13]

One particular area of the land of Israel that was especially noted for its Gentile population was that which Josephus called "the nation of the Galileans". This may be seen from Matthew 4:12–15:

> "Now when Jesus had heard that John was cast into prison, he departed into Galilee; and leaving Nazareth, he came and dwelt in Capernaum, which is upon the sea coast, in the borders of Zabulon and Nephthalim: that it might be fulfilled which was spoken by Esaias the prophet, saying, The land of Zabulon, and the land of Nephthalim, by the way of the sea, beyond Jordan, **Galilee of the Gentiles** (Gk. *éthnos*)."

During the overthrow of the nation of Israel by the Romans in AD 69/70, Galilee was one of the areas that suffered most. Josephus records the downfall of Gadara, Jotapata, Joppa, Tiberius, Taricheæ, Gamala and Gischala[14]— all towns of Galilee. In fact, Josephus was the leader of the army that vainly tried to defend Jotapata from the Roman offensive. When Jotapata was taken by siege, Josephus defected to the Romans.

It goes without saying that all the inhabitants of the abovementioned "nations" and towns — Gentiles as well as Jews — would suffer at the hands of the Romans. This I believe to be adequate explanation for the use by the Lord of the expression "distress **of nations** with perplexity".

This distress of nations was to be "with perplexity". The word "perplexity"[15] literally means 'no way out'. Jesus could not have

---

13. *The Parousia*, page 105.

14. Josephus, *Wars of the Jews*, 3:7–4:2.

15. The word "perplexity" is the Greek *aporiá*, and it is found only at Luke 21:25. W. E. Vine writes: "APORIA, ἀπορία, (Literally, 'at a loss for a way' from *a*, negative, *poros*, a way, resource); in Luke 21:25 of the distress of nations, finding no solution to their embarrassments; papyri illustrations are in the sense of being at one's wits end, at a loss how to proceed, without resources." (*Expository Dictionary of New Testament Words*, vol. 3, page 177).

It is interesting to note the use of the word "perplexity" in Micah ch. 7. The chapter speaks of the time when the Lord would go to the Israel-fig tree (for more

[Footnote continued on next page]

used a better word. Once the Romans had besieged the towns of Galilee, there was literally no way out. The inhabitants had to resign themselves to their fate.

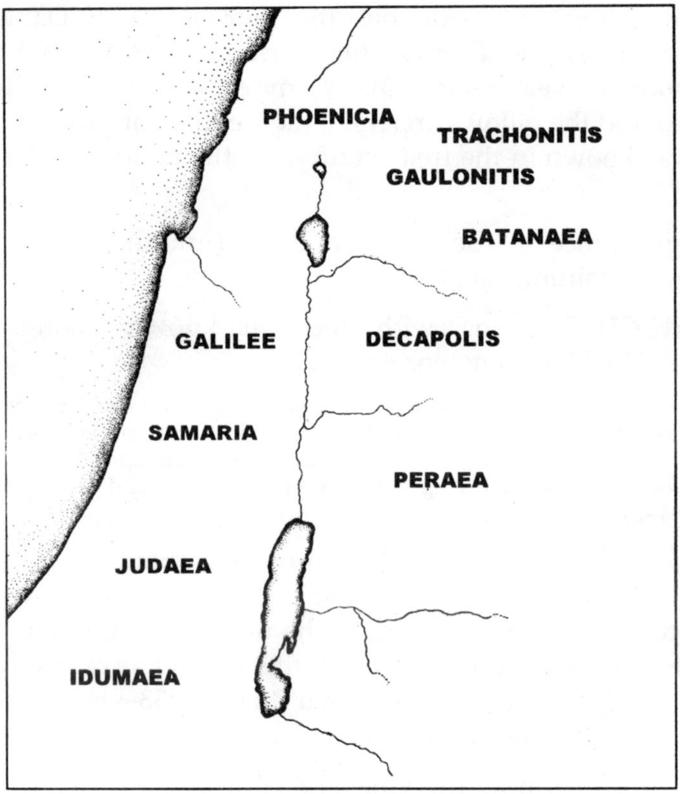

The nations of the land of Palestine at the time of AD 70

Jesus says that the nations will be in perplexity because of "the roaring of the sea and the billows" (RV), in other words, the

on the Israel-fig tree see chapter 8) looking for fruit — "my soul desireth the firstripe fig" (v.1 RV). All he found were briers and thorns (v.4; cf. Matt. 7:16–19 and especially 2 Sam. 23:6,7 AVm). Therefore, says God, "The day of thy watchmen and thy visitation cometh". In saying this He speaks of the punishment of the nation at the hand of the Roman armies in AD 70. Of this, God says, "Now shall be their *perplexity*" (v.4).

roaring of the sea and the billows is the reason for the perplexity. To what, then does "the sea and the billows" refer?

The sea in Scripture is used from time to time as a symbol of the Gentile nations. For example, the four beasts of Daniel ch. 7, which represent the four Gentile world empires are said to come "up **from the sea**" (Dan. 7:3). We may, therefore, conclude that "the sea and the billows" refers to the Gentile nations of the world as it was known in the first century, i.e. the nations of the Roman Empire.

The significance of "the **roaring** of the sea and the billows" will be seen by examining Isaiah ch. 5:

ISAIAH CH. 5 opens with the well-known "Song of the Vineyard" which commences:

> "My wellbeloved hath a vineyard in a very fruitful hill: And he fenced it, and gathered out the stones thereof, and planted it with the choicest vine, and built a tower in the midst of it, and also made a winepress therein: and he looked that it should bring forth grapes, and it brought forth wild grapes." (vv.1–2)

On two separate occasions, this prophecy about the vineyard of Israel appears to have formed the basis for parables of Jesus. The first occasion was the parable of the unfruitful fig tree planted in the vineyard (Luke 13:6–9); and the second occasion was the parable of the wicked husbandmen (Matt. 21:33–46). Both of these parables are prophecies of AD 70.

Isaiah describes how the vineyard brought forth "wild grapes". What then could the owner of the vineyard do? "I will take away the hedge thereof, and it shall be eaten up; and break down the wall thereof, and it shall be **trodden down**" (v.5). In the light of what follows it surely is no coincidence that in Luke 21:24, Jesus said, "Jerusalem shall be **trodden down** of the Gentiles, until the times of the Gentiles be fulfilled."

The Roman invasion commenced this period of Jerusalem's downtreading. It is, therefore, fitting that Isaiah continues to prophesy of the gathering together of the Roman armies against Israel: "And he will lift up an ensign to the nations **from far**, and will hiss unto them **from the end of the earth:** and, behold, they shall come with speed **swiftly**" (v.26). Isaiah is clearly referring back to Moses' prophecy in Deuteronomy ch. 28 (which is also a prophecy of AD 70), "The LORD shall bring a nation against thee **from far, from the end of the earth,** as **swift** as the eagle flieth; a nation whose tongue thou shalt not understand" (Deut. 28:49).

Concerning this gathering of the nations against Israel, Isaiah continues:

> "Their roaring shall be like a lion, they shall roar like young lions: yea, they shall roar, and lay hold of the prey, and carry it away safe, and there shall be none to deliver. And they shall roar against them in that day **like the roaring of the sea.**" (vv. 29–30 RV)

The "roaring of the sea and the billows" was thus the coming of the Romans in judgement against Israel in AD 66/70. As a result of this "roaring of the sea and the billows", the nation of Israel was destroyed. Isaiah, therefore, continues: "And if one look unto the **land** (Heb. *'erets* = 'earth'), behold darkness and **distress,**[16] and the **light is darkened in the clouds** (AV "heavens") thereof" (v.30 RV). We may set out these words of Isaiah ch. 5 in parallel with those of Jesus in Luke 21:25.

ISAIAH 5:30 (RV)	LUKE 21:25 (RV)
And they shall roar against them in that day like the roaring of the sea...	The roaring of the sea and the billows ...
And if one look unto the land [Heb. *'erets* = 'earth' or 'land'] behold darkness and distress... (LXX has "perplexity")	And upon the earth (Gk. *gē* = 'land' or 'earth') distress of nations, in perplexity...
And the light is darkened in the clouds (AV "heavens") thereof...	And there shall be signs in sun and moon and stars...

This confirms the exposition that we have set forth that the "distress of nations" was to take place **in the land of Israel**.

16. The LXX has *aporía*, "perplexity" (same word as in Luke 21:25), at this point.

Jesus continues in Luke 21 to say that "men's hearts" will be "failing them for fear, and for looking after those things which are coming on the earth" (Gk. *oikoumēne*) (v.26). Seen in its context, it is clear that this verse has nothing to do with the worldwide fear of terrorism, or of biological and nuclear weapons of mass destruction and their sophisticated delivery systems that understandably trouble people of the 21st century.

It is important to notice that here the word "earth" *(Gk. oikoumēne)* is not the same as the word translated "earth" in verse 25 where the Greek word is *gē*. The word *oikoumēne* means 'the inhabited earth', and has reference to the then known world — that is, the Roman Empire. It is, of course, true to say that the nation of Israel was part of the Roman Empire and, therefore, would share in the dreadful things "coming on the earth".

The years leading up to AD 70 constituted a time of great unrest and upheaval for the whole of the Roman Empire. At this point the reader might care to look back at the comments on pages 21–25, especially the quotation from *Tacitus: The Histories*, on page 23. As Jesus had predicted, nation fought against nation, kingdom against kingdom, and there were great wars and commotions throughout the Roman Empire (Luke 21:9, 10). These international events would strike terror into the hearts of all men and, as those events centred on Israel unfolded, especially into the hearts of the inhabitants of that land. The Jewish people shared in the experience of those in other parts of the troubled empire as the Roman legions set about their work of seeking to restore order. As the unstoppable tide of the Roman armies poured over the land of Judaea, engulfing and visiting with destruction every city and village in their path, it is no exaggeration to say that the hearts of their inhabitants would fail for fear.

4. The Sign of the Son of Man in Heaven

The Lord proceeds, in Matthew 24:30, to say, "And **then** shall appear the sign of the Son of man in heaven..." The sign that the Son of man was in heaven is thus linked by the context to events described previously, i.e. to the destruction of the heavens and earth of Israel.[17]

Jesus a short while later said to the Jewish council, "Hereafter shall **ye** see the Son of man sitting on the right hand of power, and coming in the clouds of heaven" (Matt. 26:64). He was speaking to the rebellious Jews, and referring to Psalm 110:1 — "The LORD said unto my Lord, Sit thou at my right hand." He was telling them that they were going to see it! **They, the Sanhedrin,** would see Jesus exalted to God's right hand; **they, the Sanhedrin**, would see Jesus coming in the clouds of heaven. It is clear that this "coming" cannot refer to the Lord's second coming for which we wait, for, even if it is argued that these Jews of the Sanhedrin will be raised from the dead, they will not see him in **the act of coming**. Jesus comes before the dead are raised. In what sense, then, did they see Jesus exalted to the right hand of power? In what sense did they see him coming?

This is what Jesus is talking about in the Olivet Prophecy. The Jews did not **literally** see Jesus sitting on the right hand of power — what they saw was **the sign** that Jesus had been thus exalted.[18] The destruction of Jerusalem, the passing away of Israel's heavens and earth, was the sign that the Jesus whom they

---

17. Many maintain that the *sign of the Son of man in heaven* "will be a literal sight in the sky. The sight will be the Son of man himself as he comes to the earth..." (H. A. Whittaker, *The Last Days*, page 52). There are two problems with this: (1) It is contrary to the normal use of language to speak of *a sign* of a happening as if it were the happening itself (see footnote 19 below). (2) It ignores the fact that the time context demands that it be associated with the dissolution of Israel's commonwealth.

18. "***The sign of the Son of man in heaven*** — then shall the Son of man give a proof of himself, whom they would not before acknowledge: a proof, indeed, not in any visible figure, but in vengeance and judgement so visible, that all the tribes of the earth would be forced to acknowledge him the avenger... Many times they asked him for a *sign:* now a *sign* shall appear, that he is the true Messias, whom they despised, derided, and crucified, namely, his signal vengeance and fury such as never any nation felt..." (J. Lightfoot, *Commentary on the New Testament from the Talmud and Hebraica*, vol. 2, page 320.)

had crucified, had been raised from the dead and exalted to heaven.[19]

5. The Tribes of the Earth Mourn

Jesus is not talking in this verse about his disciples. He is talking about the Jews. "Then shall all the tribes of the earth (i.e. the land) mourn (because of the judgements), and **they** shall see the Son of man coming..." **The disciples** would know that Jesus had come in judgement when they saw the Roman eagles coming to prey upon the carcase of Israel. But not until Jerusalem collapsed would the sickening truth dawn upon **the Jews** who had rejected Jesus, that the Lord had come against them in judgement. Many would then remember the words of the Lord Jesus to the Sanhedrin — "**Ye shall see** the Son of man coming in the clouds of heaven". They were men who, unlike Saul of Tarsus, continued to kick against the pricks right to the bitter end and consequently perished in their sins.

Jeremiah ch. 4 is interesting in this connection. Jeremiah, too, speaks of the desolation of Israel — "I beheld the earth, and, lo, it was without form, and void; and the heavens, and they had no light... the cities thereof were broken down at **the presence of the LORD**, and by his fierce anger" (vv.23, 26). He too, speaks of the

---

19. H. Fowler comments: "*Then shall appear the sign*, but Jesus does not indicate where it would be seen. He certainly did not affirm that the sign would be in heaven because *in heaven* does not modify *sign*, but *the Son of man.* It is not, as many believe, *the sign in heaven*, but *the Son of man in heaven*. What does appear will indicate (= *sign*-ify) the presence of *the Son of man in heaven*.

"But is this a genitive of apposition or a genitive of source?

"**(1) Genitive of apposition:** *The sign* which is *the Son of man* in heaven. Some argue that Christ is His own self-evidencing sign. But, if the appearance of the Son of God in the sky were the sign then Jesus would be using the word *sign* in a way foreign to every other normal meaning of this term. Normally a *sign* substitutes for the object to which it points, so how could he himself be *the sign*, when his own personal appearance is supposedly the reality to be pointed out?

"**(2) Genitive of source:** *The sign* comes from, or is given by, *the Son of man in heaven*, sent by him to indicate something to men. This is the conventional use of the term and the preferable interpretation." (*The Gospel of Matthew*, vol. 4, page 483).

mourning of the tribes of the earth because of the judgements — "For this shall the **earth mourn**" (v.28).

On the occasion of which Jeremiah speaks, Jehovah came against them, manifest in the Babylonian armies, and, speaking of these armies, the prophet says, "He (the Babylonian) shall come up **as clouds**" (v.13). Thus the armies of Babylon, coming as clouds, were God's armies coming to pour out his judgements — they constituted therefore "the clouds of heaven".[20]

So with the Roman invasion in AD 70 — it was the sign to the Jews that the Son of man was in heaven, exalted to God's right hand. It caused the tribes of the land of Israel to mourn. It was the coming of the Son of man against Israel in the Roman clouds of heaven, as Jehovah had come against their fathers in the Babylonian.[21]

When Jesus, manifest in the Roman armies, came to visit Israel with judgement he came "with power and great glory" (Matt. 24:30). There are those who maintain that these words are so exalted in tone that they must refer to the future advent of the Lord. That he will come with power and great glory in the future is not disputed (e.g. Matt. 25:31). But the Lord's power and glory then will be no different from that power and glory which he

---

20. "The clouds of heaven" = the clouds of God. There is a similar use of the word "heaven" in Luke 20:4 — "The baptism of John, was it from heaven, or of men?" Here "heaven" clearly stands for "God".

21. The success of the Jews against Cestius Gallus in AD 66 (see page 40) and the withdrawal of Vespasian in AD 68 (see page 41) gave them a false sense of security. They thought that this was a sign that Jehovah was exerting himself on their behalf for the protection of Jerusalem and the Temple. One writer comments: "That such men should continue to remain as the defenders of a city upon which a relentless enemy was steadily closing in is not consistent with the character of mere brigands and desperadoes... but it clearly points to men animated, fanatically perhaps, but genuinely, with a dynamic belief that they were waging a holy war, in which they could be certain of divine help." (S. G. F. Brandon, *The Fall of Jerusalem*, page 163).

The fall of Jerusalem would have brought home to the Jews that they were wrong. Jehovah was not exerting himself on their behalf. They would be compelled to face the sickening truth that he had sent the Romans against them to pour out his judgements upon them — exactly as Jesus had said he would.

revealed in his judgement of Israel, although it will take a different form. It was at his resurrection that he entered "into his **glory**" (Luke 24:26). Also he was "declared to be the Son of God with **power**... by the resurrection from the dead" (Rom. 1:4). Thus both power and glory were given to him then. He demonstrated his possession of this power and glory by the destruction of Jerusalem and the judgement of Israel in the events surrounding AD 70.

6. The Angels Gather the Elect

On a number of occasions in the prophets, side by side with the prediction of the judgement of the nation of Israel, there is reference made to the bringing in of the Gentiles into God's redemptive plan. Although there was some overlap, and Gentiles began to be called before Jerusalem fell to the Romans, the destruction of Jerusalem marked the final end of the Mosaic dispensation and the beginning of the age of Gentile opportunity. This we saw to be the teaching of Joel 2:30–32 concerning the last days of the nation of Israel:

Judgement on Israel		Gentile opportunity
"I will show wonders in the heavens and in the earth, blood, and fire, and pillars of smoke. The sun shall be turned into darkness, and the moon into blood..." (vv. 30–31).	**JOEL 2**	"It shall come to pass, that ***whosoever*** shall call on the name of the LORD shall be delivered" (v. 32 and see Paul's use of this in Rom. 10:13).
"They shall fall by the edge of the sword, and shall be led away captive into all nations: and Jerusalem shall be trodden down of the Gentiles ..." (v.24).	**LUKE 21**	"... until the times [Gk. *kairós* = 'opportunity'][22] of the Gentiles be fulfilled" (v. 24).

[22] The word *kairós* is of uncertain derivation. Most scholars are agreed that one of its meanings is "season, or opportune time" (See J. H. Thayer, *Greek English*

It is this same teaching that lies behind the words of Jesus in Matthew 24:31. Having described, in the language of the prophets that was so familiar to the disciples, the destruction of Israel under the Mosaic system, Jesus proceeds to say, "He shall send his angels with a great sound of a trumpet, and they shall gather together his elect from the fours winds, from one end of heaven to the other". Placed in the context that we have carefully elaborated from the Scriptures, this cannot have reference to the resurrection—it has reference to events associated with the judgements of God upon Israel.

The mention of the **"great sound"** of a trumpet appears to be a reference to Numbers 10:3 where we read of the way in which various notes were blown on the two silver trumpets in order to communicate with the people. When the two trumpets were blown together, thus giving a "great sound", it was a signal for the people to gather together. So here, in the Olivet Prophecy, the sound of the trumpet "gathers together" the elect.

"The elect" who are gathered by the voice of the trumpet are the saints, having been twice mentioned already in Matthew 24:22, 24. In these previous passages "the elect" referred to are the faithful saints out of Israel. But for the most part Jesus, during his ministry, had appealed to this nation in vain. He had, therefore, rebuked them, saying, "There shall be weeping and gnashing of teeth, when ye shall see Abraham, and Isaac, and Jacob, and all the prophets, in the kingdom of God, and you yourselves thrust out." He went on to speak of the fact that the Gentiles would respond—"And they shall come from the **east**, and from the **west**, and from the **north**, and from the **south**, and shall sit down in the kingdom of God" (Luke 13:28, 29). So here, in response to the trumpet call, the elect are gathered from "the four winds", i.e. north, south, east and west—in other words, from the lands of the

---

Lexicon of the NT, page 318). This appears to be the meaning in Luke 21:24. See further comments on pages 49–50.

Gentiles.[23] This gathering together is mentioned in John 11:52, where we read that Jesus died "not for that nation (Israel) only, but that also he should **gather together** in one the children of God that were **scattered abroad**" (see also John 10:16; 12:32).

Thus Matthew 24:31 is speaking of taking out of the Gentiles a people for God's name by the mighty preaching of the gospel. This preaching was to be performed by "angels". This word does not, in itself, have reference to celestial beings. James (2:25) uses it to refer to the spies hid by Rahab who is said to have received the "messengers" (Gk. *ággelos* (pronounced *angelos*) = 'angel'). It is used in Matthew 11:10 of John the Baptist who was the "messenger" (Gk. *ággelos*) who went before Jesus. Luke 7:24 speaks of John's disciples as "messengers" (Gk. *ággelos*). So likewise here in Matthew 24:31 the "angels" who are to perform the work of gathering together the Gentiles are not to be celestial beings but the preachers of the gospel. Jesus commissioned his apostles saying, "Go ye therefore, and teach **all nations**..." (Matt. 28:19). The apostle Paul subsequently became one of these "angels". Writing to the Colossians, he said, "And be not moved away from the hope of the gospel, which ye have heard, and which was preached to **every creature which is under heaven;** whereof I Paul am made a minister" (Col. 1:23). Concerning the work of the apostles in preaching to the Gentiles, Paul, quoting from Psalm 19, says, "Their **sound** went into all the earth, and their words unto the **ends of the world**" (Gk. *oikouménē* = 'inhabited earth') (Rom. 10:18).[24]

Since AD 70, when the lights of the Israelitish heavens were extinguished and its earth was burned up, it has been mainly the

---

23. The following references will confirm that the "four winds" refer initially to the four points of the compass and that this in turn is a way of speaking about the Gentile nations — Jer. 49:36; Ezek. 12:14; 17:21; Dan. 7:2; 8:8; 11:4; Zech. 2:6.

24. Some manuscripts of the last chapter of the Gospel of Mark omit verses 9–20 as they occur in the AV and in their place have, "But they reported briefly to Peter and those with him all that they had been told. And after this, Jesus himself sent out by means of them, ***from east to west,*** the sacred and imperishable ***proclamation*** of eternal salvation" (RSV, see also NEB and Rotherham).

Gentiles, those of the four winds, who have responded to the gospel sound which has been trumpeted forth calling Gentiles and gathering them into the Ecclesia of Jesus Christ.[25]

The above may conveniently be summarised in tabular form:

THE GATHERING OF THE ELECT FROM THE FOUR WINDS	
"He shall send forth his angels…"	"***Go ye therefore,*** and teach all nations, baptizing them in the name of the Father, and of the Son, and of the Holy Spirit." (Matt. 28:19)
"With a great sound of a trumpet…"	"But I say, Have they not heard? Yes verily, ***their sound went into all the earth,*** and their words unto the ends of the world." (Rom. 10:18)
"And they shall gather together his elect…"	"And not for that nation only, but that also he ***should gather together in one the children of God*** that were scattered abroad." (John 11:52)
"From the four winds, from one end of heaven to the other."	"And they shall come ***from the east, and from the west, and from the north, and from the south***, and shall sit down in the kingdom of God." (Luke 13:29) "… be not moved away from the hope of the gospel, which ye have heard, and which ***was preached to every creature which is under heaven***…" (Col. 1:23)

[25] The importance of the events of AD 66–70 in connection with the progress of the Gospel in Gentile lands cannot be over-estimated. Paul had been arrested about AD 55. His restraining influence on the Jerusalem-led Judaizing of the Gentile congregations was, with his arrest and subsequent execution, removed. With his removal, from a human standpoint, it would appear that the Judaizers were better placed to interfere with the progress of the Truth in Gentile lands. The events of AD 66–70 changed all this. One writer observes: "In the overthrow of the Jewish state the old wine skins of Judaism were burst asunder and perished, liberating the new wine to flow freely abroad and to reach maturity in places more congenial to the original genius of its creator. Thus we may conclude that, after the Resurrection experiences, the next most crucial event in the life of the Christian Church was the overthrow of the Jewish nation, which was dramatically epitomised in the destruction of its holy city of Jerusalem in AD 70." (S. G. F. Brandon, *The Fall of Jerusalem and the Christian Church*, page 251.)

7. Your Redemption Draweth Nigh (Luke 21:28)

Some Bible students have difficulty accepting the view advanced that the Olivet Prophecy was fulfilled in its entirety in AD 70 because of the words of Luke 21:28, "And when these things begin to come to pass, then look up, and lift up your heads; for **your redemption** draweth nigh." How, it is asked, did the believers obtain any kind of "redemption" in AD 70? [26]

The Greek word translated "redemption" is *apolútrōsis*,[27] which literally means 'release for a ransom' and hence 'deliverance, liberation, redemption'. The idea of the payment of a ransom is not always involved when the word is used. For example in Hebrews 11:35 it appears simply to denote deliverance from persecution: "Women received their dead raised to life again: and others were tortured, not accepting **deliverance** (Gk. *apolútrōsis*)". This I believe to be the meaning of the word in Luke 21:28.[28] The period leading up to AD 70 was one of great affliction and

---

[26] It is only fair that alert readers to the fact that at this point I part company with esteemed Bible students who could not see how the "redemption" promised to the disciples could have been realised at any time other than at the Lord's second advent. E.g. Robert Roberts wrote: "...that generation did not pass till the things spoken of were in their proximate aspect accomplished: when the signs Jesus gave the disciples showed themselves, the destruction of the nation was nigh at hand, even at the door. It was to these events that Christ's statements primarily applied, and therefore his statements proved true in their occurrence. Redemption as growing out of them and coming after them came nigh with them, but actually was separated from them by a chronological gulf which they were confessedly not aware." (Answer to the question: "Was Redemption Nigh in the Apostolic Age?", *The Christadelphian*, 1877, page 379.) The reader will have to decide which explanation is best supported by Scripture.

[27] On this word *apolútrōsis* McClintock and Strong state: "It signifies not merely the liberation of captives but deliverance from exile, death and every other evil from which we may be freed. The nature of this redemption or purchased deliverance... is ***therefore to be ascertained by the circumstances of those who are the subjects of it.***" (*Cyclopaedia of Biblical, Theological and Ecclesiastical Literature*, vol. 8, page 972.)

[28] S. Zodhiates so understands the use of the term *apolútrōsis* in these Scriptures — "Deliverance from calamities and death without the idea of a ransom being paid (Luke 21:28; Heb. 11:35)." (*The Complete Word Study Dictionary: New Testament*, page 233.)

difficulty for the faithful Jewish brethren in those "last days". An example of this is to be found in James 5 where we read of the oppression of the faithful poor by the unfaithful rich:

> "Go to now, ye rich, weep and howl for your miseries that are coming upon you... Ye have laid up your treasure in the last days. Behold, the hire of the labourers who mowed your fields, which is of you kept back by fraud, crieth out: and the cries of them that reaped have entered into the ears of the Lord of Sabaoth... Ye have condemned, ye have killed the righteous one; he doth not resist you."

He goes on to urge the faithful to be patient. The Lord will soon visit their oppressors with judgement:

> "Be ye also patient; stablish your hearts: for the coming of the Lord is at hand." (James 5:1-8 RV)[29]

These experiences of the apostles and other persecuted saints were predicted in the Olivet Prophecy, as we have seen (e.g. Luke 21:16). This is why Jesus gave them the parable of the Unjust Judge in Luke ch. 18.[30] The Lord came and avenged the poor widow (i.e. the faithful believers) — the "elect" — by bringing judgement upon their enemies. This was their "deliverance" or "redemption".

This promised redemption was said to be "nigh at hand" and it is of interest to note that the word translated "nigh at hand", (*eggízō*, pronounced, *engizo*), is used on a number of occasions in connection with the events of AD 70. In this same chapter the Lord warns, "When ye shall see Jerusalem compassed with armies, then know that the desolation thereof is nigh (Gk. *eggízō*)" (Luke 21:20). Later the apostle Peter who also warns of the impending overthrow of Israel writes, "The end of all things is at hand (Gk. *eggízō*): be ye therefore sober, and watch unto prayer" (1 Pet. 4:7). Also, as noted above, James who seeks to encourage the oppressed faithful in "the last days", writes of the imminent

---

29. More on this on page 98.

30. It is of more than passing interest that the context of this parable (i.e. the discourse in Ch. 17:22–37) is very similar to the final section of the Olivet Prophecy.

coming of the Lord in judgement against their oppressors, "Be ye also patient; stablish your hearts: for the coming of the Lord is at hand (Gk. *eggízō*)" (James 5:8 RV).

Finally it should be noted that Jesus said, "And when **these things**[31] **begin** to come to pass, then look up, and lift up your heads; for your redemption draweth nigh" (Luke 21:28). That the beginning of the things discussed in the Olivet Prophecy has reference to the events leading up to AD 70 cannot be denied. Therefore, it follows that the "redemption", which is tied by the context to the **beginning** of those events, was achieved by the AD 70 judgements. It refers to the deliverance of the early believers, especially the Jewish believers, from the oppression visited upon them by their unbelieving contemporaries.

An artist's impression of the conquest of Jerusalem

31. Note this phrase in the disciples' question in Luke 21:7 — "What sign will there be when ***these things*** shall come to pass?"

CHAPTER EIGHT

THE PARABLE OF THE FIG TREE

Matthew 24

32 Now learn a parable of
the fig tree; When his
branch is yet tender, and
putteth forth leaves, ye
know that summer is nigh:
33 So likewise ye, when ye
shall see all these things,
know that it is near, even at
the doors. 34 Verily I say
unto you, This generation
shall not pass, till all these
things be fulfilled.

Mark 13

28 Now learn a parable of
the fig tree; When her
branch is yet tender, and
putteth forth leaves, ye
know that summer is near:
29 So ye in like manner,
when ye shall see these
things come to pass, know
that it is nigh, even at the
doors. 30 Verily I say unto
you, that this generation
shall not pass, till all these
things be done.

Luke 21

29 And he spake to them a
parable; Behold the fig tree,
and all the trees; 30 When
they now shoot forth, ye
see and know of your own
selves that summer is now
nigh at hand. 31 So like-wise
ye, when ye see these
things come to pass, know
ye that the kingdom of God
is nigh at hand. 32 Verily I
say unto you, This gener-
ation shall not pass away,
till all be fulfilled.

In Matthew 24:32 Jesus gives a parable to his disciples: "Now learn a parable of the fig tree; When his branch is yet tender, and putteth forth leaves, ye know that summer is nigh: so likewise ye, when ye see all these things, know that it is near, even at the doors" (vv. 32, 33).

The Simple Message

There is a simple message in the parable which must not be overlooked. Just as the tender branch and the leaves on the fig tree herald the approach of summer, so the signs of those times, as they were observed by the disciples, would herald the coming judgement. As they saw the wars, the famines, the abomination of desolation, so they would know that the end of Israel's existence as a nation was at hand. We may set this out diagrammatically in a way which provides a time context for the interpretation of the parable of the fig tree:

THE LORD'S MOUNT OLIVET PROPHECY

THE DISCIPLES' QUESTION		
Tell	***us***	When shall these things be?
JESUS' REPLY		
	Ye	shall hear of wars…
Take heed that no man deceive	***you***	
See that	***ye***	be not troubled…
They shall deliver	***you***	up to be afflicted…
And	***ye***	shall be hated of all men…
When	***ye***	therefore see the abomination that maketh desolate…
Pray	***ye***	that your flight be not in the winter…
If any man shall say unto	***you***	Lo, here is Christ, believe it not…
I have told	***you***	beforehand…
Wherefore if they say unto	***you***	Behold, he is in the desert; go not forth…
Now learn a parable of the fig tree. When his branch is tender and putteth forth leaves	***ye***	know that summer is nigh.
So likewise	***ye***	
when	***ye***	see all these things, know that it is near, even at the doors.
Verily, I say unto	***You***	This generation shall not pass, till all these things be fulfilled.

From this we see that the parable of the fig tree and the warning concerning that generation is inextricably linked by the context to those very disciples who asked the question in the first place.

This simple teaching is overlooked by those who seek to press these verses of the Olivet Prophecy into supporting the imminence of the second advent.[1] First an assumption is made

[1] Our early prophetic writers consistently saw in the parable of the fig tree a reference to the development of the signs of which Jesus had earlier spoken indicative of the approach of Israel's AD 70 judgement. (See footnote 9, page 98.) Even in the significant period that saw the foundation of the Zionist Organisation in 1897 and the Balfour Declaration in 1917, when the development of Zionism was followed with very great interest, in *The Christadelphian*

[Footnote continued on next page]

that in the parable of the fig tree Jesus is speaking about Israel in the latter days—"When the Jewish people, after nearly 2,000 years of exile, under relentless persecution, became a nation again on May 14th 1948 the 'fig tree' put forth its first leaves."[2] Then, on

---

magazine there was no application in its pages, in editorials or articles, of the parable of the fig tree to those significant events.

In fact the earliest application of the parable to Zionism that I have been able to find in *The Christadelphian*, was in 1925. Under the heading of "Watchman, What of the Night?" the writer comments, "The time to favour Zion has come. The special sign of our Lord's coming, graciously given by him to his loved ones in compliance with their request, is now under observation in the political heaven, in 'Zionism.' We now behold the political buds of Zionism 'shooting forth,' which is a clear indication of approaching harvest. The 'sign of the coming of the Son of Man' is here." [It is pertinent to note that this was written in 1925.] The writer continued: "This generation — the generation which is privileged to see these soul stirring events, which our eyes now behold, shall not pass away till all be fulfilled." (G. Waite, "Watchman, What of the Night?", *The Christadelphian*, vol. 62, page 17). The passage of time has shown that anticipation to be without foundation.

The application of the parable of the fig tree to the modern revival of Israel appears to have been accepted uncritically from the writings of those whose understanding of "the things concerning the Kingdom of God" was questionable, to say the least. The earliest application of the parable to the restoration of Israel that I have been able to find is that by H. Alford, in 1867, who wrote, "The putting forth of the fig tree from the state of its winter dryness, symbolizes the future reviviscence of that race, which the Lord declares shall not pass away till all be fulfilled" (*The New Testament for English Readers*, vol. 1, page 169). [On Alford's identification of the "generation that shall not pass" with the Jewish race, see footnote 15, page 101.]

In preparing this Second Edition I came across the following interesting quotation by C. T. Russell, the founder of the Watchtower Bible and Tract Society. It was written in 1897, the year the first Zionist Congress was held: "The fig tree in this prophecy may be understood to signify the Jewish nation. If so, it is being signally fulfilled; for not only are thousands of Israelites returning to Palestine, but the Zionist movement, as all know, has now assumed such proportions as to justify Conventions of representatives from all parts of the world to meet year by year to put in practical shape the proposal for the reorganisation of a Jewish state in Palestine. These buds will thrive***, but will bear no perfect fruit before October 1914 – the full end of Gentile Times.***" (*Studies in the Scriptures*, vol. 4, page 604. [Emphasis mine, JA].) Again the passage of time showed the theory to be unfounded, and perhaps this was one of the reasons that led the Watchtower Bible and Tract Society to reject the regathering of the Jews as being a fulfilment of Bible prophecy.

2. H. Lindsey, *The Late Great Planet Earth*, page 53.

the basis of this assumption, the budding of the fig tree is assumed to be a sign of Christ's return, as in the following: "A budding and shooting fig tree must represent a national resurgence after a period of dormancy—such as we are witnessing today... Jesus said the budding of the fig tree was a sign of his return. This is why for true Christians the formation of the State of Israel is such a wonderful event."[3]

But did not Jesus indicate that the generation to witness the budding of the fig tree would not pass until all be fulfilled? The generation that saw the creation of the State of Israel—taking a generation as a period of about 40 years[4] — ended in 1988. The fact that Jesus has not returned suggests that such explanations of the Lord's words are fundamentally flawed.[5]

---

3. Peter. J. Southgate, *Light On Israel*, (Light Magazine, vol. 6.1), page 18.

The foundation of the State of Israel is indeed a wonderful event. But the reason for believing that it is important rests on a much firmer foundation than that provided by this interpretation of the parable of the fig tree. It is interesting to note that in what might be referred to as 'foundation works' (e.g. John Thomas, *Elpis Israel* [1848], R. Roberts, *Christendom Astray* [1869], T. Williams, *The World's Redemption* [1913], J. Carter, *God's Way* [1948]) which are very forthright in their anticipation of the regathering of the Jews, I have been unable to locate a single reference to the parable of the fig tree. E. Humphreys states the prevailing view of these early Bible students when he writes, "Any attempt to interpret the parable of the fig tree with reference to the restoration of Israel in our day does injustice to the Lord's language" (*Testimony*, vol. 47, page 128).

4. This is the generally agreed period: "*Geneá* (γενεά)... especially of those of the Jewish race living at the same period, Matt. 11:16 etc. Transferred from people to the time in which they lived, the word came to mean an age, i.e. a period ordinarily occupied by each successive generation, say, of thirty or forty years" (W. E. Vine, *Expository Dictionary of New Testament Words*, vol. 1, page 42).

5. As so often happens when predictions which are based on flimsy evidence fail to materialise, the 'goal posts' of interpretation are moved. The foundation of the Zionist Movement marked by the holding of the first Zionist Congress in 1897 (e.g. C. T. Russell, writing in 1897, see footnote 1 above; P. Perret, *Prophecies I Have Seen Fulfilled*", written in 1938); the early work of the Zionists (e.g. G. Waite writing in *The Christadelphian* 1925, page 17, see footnote 1 above); the removal of the Turk from Jerusalem in 1917 (e.g. S. Schorr, writing in 1933, *The Everlasting Nation and Their Coming King*, page 77); and the foundation of the State of Israel in 1948 (e.g. H. Lindsey, *The Late Great Planet Earth*, page 53)—

[Footnote continued on next page]

But there may be more to this parable of the fig tree than the simple message. First we note what many have observed – that the parable is rich in its allusions to the Old Testament and, in this connection, Joel ch. 1 and Micah ch. 7 are particularly helpful.

JOEL 1: When the Assyrian invaded Judah in the days of Hezekiah, his armies swept over the land of Judah like a swarm of locusts, destroying all the fenced cities. The desolation of Judah at that time is described by God through the prophet: "A nation is come up upon my land… He hath laid my vine waste, and barked **my fig tree**: he hath made it clean bare, and cast it away; the branches thereof are made white" (vv. 6, 7).

MICAH 7: We have already had reason to refer to this prophecy, which is so rich in its allusions to the ministry of Jesus. The work of the Lord as he went to Israel, on behalf of his Father, looking for fruit is described: "Woe is me! for I am as when they have gathered the summer fruits, as the grape gleanings of the vintage: there is no cluster to eat: my soul desireth **the firstripe fig**" (v.1 RV). But there was so little fruit to be found. Interestingly, we observe that this fig tree was in a vineyard, and so Jesus, with obvious reference to this scripture, in the parable in Luke ch. 13

---

have all been used as the starting point of the 40 years of ***"this generation"*** that would see "all things" fulfilled.

So now, 1988 having come and gone, we read, "The Israeli fig tree truly sprouted with buds in 1948 when the State of Israel was reborn, ***but*** was clothed with leaves when Jerusalem was proclaimed its Capital in 1967 and the millions of Jews returned from the nations where they had been dispersed. It is ***becoming obvious*** that the ***"generation"*** spoken of, generally accepted as a period of 40 years, is that generation which saw the mighty events of 1967." (*Present Day Events Report*, March 1996.) Another, writing in 1992, offers the following, "The fig tree parable refers to the beginnings of ***Jewish repentance*** in the last days which will herald the establishment of the Kingdom at Christ's return." (D. Heaster, *The Last Days*, page 189.) [Emphasis mine throughout, JA]

In view of this evident failure to successfully identify ***this generation*** we therefore commend the words of H. Fowler in this respect: "No objective reading of this paragraph (Matt. 24:32–34) will justify the creation of an allegory of the rebirth of the Jewish State without reading into Jesus' words what is not there, to favour a preconceived theory of eschatology" (*The Gospel of Matthew*, vol. 4, page 505).

spoke of a certain man who planted a fig tree "in his vineyard", and "came and sought fruit thereon, and found none" (Luke 13:6). The prophet Micah continues to describe this barrenness of Israel — "The good man is perished out of the earth: and there is none upright among men… The best of them is as a brier: the most upright is sharper than a thorn hedge" (vv. 2, 4). Again, we see this reflected in the teaching of Jesus when he said, "Do men gather grapes of thorns, or figs of thistles?" (Matt. 7:16). Thus he continued in his parable in Luke ch.13 to speak of his ministry — "Behold, these three years I come seeking fruit on this fig tree, and find none: cut it down; why cumbereth it the ground?" (Luke 13:7).

Thus both Joel ch. 1 and Micah ch. 7 unite to tell us that in the Old Testament the nation of Israel is spoken of as a fig tree.

"A certain man had a fig tree planted in his vineyard; and he came seeking fruit thereon, and found none… let it alone this year also, till I shall dig about it, and dung it: and if it bear fruit thenceforth, well: but if not, thou shalt cut it down" (Luke 13:6-7 (RV)

The Cursing of the Fig Tree

This Old Testament background, and the application made of it by Jesus in his teaching, combine together to help us appreciate the miracle of the cursing of the fig tree recorded in Matthew ch. 21. This miracle, as were many if not all of the Lord's miracles, was an acted parable. The fig tree, which on the basis of what we have already seen represented the nation of Israel, is said to have been "in **the way**" (v.19). This phrase is full of meaning,[6] and denotes that this fig tree nation of Israel was a favoured nation indeed. They were God's covenant people called to rejoice in his mercy and his truth. It was reasonable, therefore, that Jesus should come to the tree seeking fruit — i.e. evidence of a faithful response to the truth. But there was no fruit to be found on the Israel fig tree, "but leaves only". Mark adds: "the time of figs was not yet" (Mark 11:13). It was the time when "the fig tree shall not blossom, neither shall fruit be in the vines" (Hab. 3:17). There could be no fruit in a nation that rejected God's own Son, and the "time of figs" will only come when the nation accepts him — the time of which Isaiah speaks when, "The remnant that is escaped of the house of Judah shall again take root downward,[7] and bear fruit upward" (Isa. 37:31).

Because there was no fruit to be had, Jesus cursed the fig tree with the words, "May no fruit grow on thee to the Age (Gk. *eis ton aiōna*)" (Matt. 21:19 *Emphatic Diaglott*).

---

6. The significance of the phrase as denoting a people with whom God had a special relationship is seen by observing that: The generation of Noah's day "corrupted ***[God's] way***" (Gen. 6:12); Abraham and his seed were commended because they would faithfully "keep ***the way*** of the LORD" (Gen.18:19); Israel was to be looked over by an angel which would "keep [them] in ***the way***" (Exod. 23:20); the believers in the Acts record are said to be "of ***the Way***" (Acts 9:2; 19:9 RV).

7. Note that in Mark's record of the cursing of the fig tree it is said that "they saw the fig tree dried up ***from the roots***" (Mark 11:20).

The Fig Tree

The next morning, which was the same day on which the Olivet Prophecy was given, the disciples, returning from Bethany to Jerusalem, were amazed to see that the fig tree had "withered away" (Matt. 21:18, 20).

What has all this to do with the parable of the fig tree in Matthew ch. 24? Surely this miracle of the cursing of the fig tree, which was fresh in the minds of the disciples, is that to which Jesus was directing their attention when he said, "From **the** fig tree (Gk. *tēs sukēs*) learn her parable" (v.32 RV); i.e. from that same fig tree which I cursed and which only this morning you beheld withered up—from **that** fig tree learn her parable.

All the Trees

In Luke's version of the parable, we read, "Behold the fig tree, and **all the trees**; When they shoot forth, ye see and know of your own selves that summer is now nigh at hand" (Luke 21:29, 30). A number of Bible students see in the phrase "all the trees" a reference to the Arab nations surrounding Israel. For example, one writer comments:

> "*Behold the fig tree and all the trees* — This century which has seen Israel re-established has also seen the same kind of remarkable political revival, though for vastly different reasons, in the nations which surround Israel. Oil and the rivalries of the super-powers have given the Arab neighbours surrounding Israel a political consciousness and importance which it was beyond the power of any 19th Century student of Bible prophecy to foresee."[8]

Perhaps here is another example of the expositor's wish being the father of his thoughts. It would be difficult to sustain this conclusion by scripturally reasoned argument.

An alternative explanation of Luke's additional words, in harmony with the time context of the Olivet Prophecy, is arrived

---

[8] H. A. Whittaker, *Studies in the Gospels*, page 612. Others argue along the same lines but do not confine the other trees to the Arabs. E.g. T. Benson, "Under the latter day interpretation these are the other nations which, like Israel, have become independent in modern times" (*Testimony*, vol. 66, page 82).

at by observing that in the Old Testament Israel is spoken of as an olive tree (Jer. 11:16); a vine (Psalm 80:8); and a cedar (Ezek. 17:22,23). "The fig tree and all the trees" would appear to be an invitation to consider Israel as mentioned by the prophets in these various ways. It is also interesting to note that Joel in the chapter already referred to in which Israel is spoken of as God's vine and fig tree, uses the very words employed by the Lord in Luke 21:29 when, concerning the Assyrian invasion of Israel he says, "The vine is dried up, and the fig tree languisheth; the pomegranate tree, the palm tree also, and the apple tree, even **all the trees** of the field, are withered…" (Joel 1:12).

John the Baptist confirms this approach when, speaking of the impending judgement of Israel, he said, "The axe is laid unto the root of **the trees**" (Matt. 3:10).

Leaves Only

The fig tree that Jesus cursed had "leaves only". It had no fruit. So also in the Olivet Prophecy Jesus directed them to consider the Israel-fig tree at a time when there were leaves but no fruit—it "putteth forth leaves" (Matt. 24:32), just as was the case with the fig tree that he had recently cursed. As the signs of the times, of which Jesus had been speaking, gradually unfolded, the nation of Israel would continue to be a barren nation. An external show of religion would continue to be evident, but no real fruit to God would be produced. In fact, this external show of religion, their zeal for God not according to knowledge (the foliage of the Israel-fig tree) would produce some of the signs of the times in the form of rejection and persecution of the believers, and the emergence of false messiahs and false prophets. The continual development of this foliage and absence of fruit would herald the coming of the judge.

At the Doors

Thus the disciples learned the lesson of **the** fig tree. The Olivet Prophecy was a detailed description of the withering of the fig tree of Israel. As they beheld the signs developing within that nation according to the prediction of the Lord, so they would know that the coming of Jesus against Israel in judgement was near—they would know that "he is nigh, even at the doors" (Matt. 24:33 RV).[9]

It is interesting to see how James in his letter takes hold of this and applies it to the Jewish brethren prior to AD 70, thus confirming the application of the Olivet Prophecy to that period of time. He is writing to Jews (ch. 1:1), and in chapter 5 rebukes the unfaithful and rebellious rich for the way in which they have treated the poor, and encourages the poor with the message that the judge of Israel is near.[10] The following points should be noted:

1. To the unfaithful rich he says, "Ye have laid up your treasure in the **last days**" (v.3 RV). Thus those days were, as we have previously showed, the last days of the nation of Israel.
2. He encourages the faithful with the words, "Be patient therefore brethren, until the **coming** of the Lord" (v.7 RV). He uses the same word for the coming of the Lord as that used by the disciples when they asked, "What shall be the sign of thy coming (Gk. *parousia* = 'presence') and the end of the age?" Thus James here is concerned with the same period as that dealt with in the Olivet Prophecy—the end of the age, or the last days of Israel—which will see the presence of the Lord in judgement. He announces, "Be ye... patient... for the coming of the Lord **is at hand**" (v. 8 RV).
3. James wrote his letter some considerable time after the Olivet Prophecy was given. Many of the signs of the times of which Jesus spoke had already been witnessed by the faithful, and, in fact, James' letter considers some of them. Thus, as the

---

9. So, John Thomas: "The fig tree is a symbol of the Jewish nation planted and cultivated in Judaea. In the days of Jesus, the branch was yet tender and it put forth leaves, showing that its life was not extinct... As, then, they knew of the approach of summer by the shooting of the leaves, so might they know of the approach of the desolation, when ***they*** beheld the results he had detailed in the first 28 verses (of Matt. 24). ("The Mount Olivet Prophecy", *Herald of the Kingdom and Age to Come*, vol. 10, page 277.)

10. There are echoes here of the parable of the Unjust Judge (Luke 18:1–8).

judgements of AD 70 fast approach, he takes up the words of Jesus in the parable of the fig tree, and says to the faithful, "Murmur not, brethren, one against another, that ye be not judged: behold, **the judge standeth before the doors**" (v.9 RV).

The wrath of the Lord was about to be poured out — then!

The Kingdom of God is Nigh

Luke records the interpretation to the parable of the fig tree as follows: "So likewise ye, when ye see these things come to pass, know ye that **the kingdom of God** is nigh at hand" (Luke 22:31). This presents difficulties in the minds of some. In what sense could it possibly be said that the kingdom of God was "nigh at hand" in AD 70?

The phrase "the kingdom of God" is one that is used on several occasions by Luke with reference to Jesus himself:

> "Heal the sick that are therein, and say unto them, The kingdom of God is come nigh unto you." (Luke 10:9)
>
> "But if I with the finger of God cast out devils, no doubt the kingdom of God is come upon you." (Luke 11:20)
>
> "The kingdom of God cometh not with observation: Neither shall they say, Lo (Gk. *idoú* = 'behold') here! or, lo there! for, behold, the kingdom of God is within you ('among you' AVm)."[11] (Luke 17:20,21)

A comparison of the records of Jesus' entry into Jerusalem, just prior to his crucifixion, also indicates that "the kingdom of God" was used by the Jews to refer to the Messiah, the King of the Kingdom. Notice what the multitudes shouted, as recorded by Mark and Luke, as they welcomed Jesus:

---

[11] The kingdom was certainly not "within" those sinful Pharisees to whom Jesus was speaking. He declared of them, "Ye are like unto whited sepulchres, which indeed appear beautiful outward, but are within full of dead men's bones, and of all uncleanness" (Matt. 23:27). He appears to be referring to that phenomenon which would be increasingly characteristic of them as one of the signs of their times. Namely, that sign concerning which he warned his disciples in the prophecy under consideration — "If they shall say unto you, Behold (Gk. *idoú*), he is in the desert; go not forth: behold, he is in the secret chambers; believe it not" (Matt. 24:26). The Pharisees would look in deserts and secret places for a deliverer; but if only they had opened their eyes they would have seen him then — amongst them!

Luke 19:38	Mark 11:10
"Blessed be **the king** that cometh in the name of the Lord."	"Blessed be **the kingdom** of our father David, that cometh in the name of the Lord."

In fact, we need go no further than the Olivet Prophecy to show that "the kingdom of God" in Luke 21:31 refers to Jesus himself. We see this by comparing the two accounts in Matthew and Luke:

Matthew 24:33 (RV)	Luke 21:31
"So likewise ye, when ye see these things, know ye that **he is nigh,** even at the doors."	"So likewise ye, when ye see these things come to pass, know ye that **the kingdom of God is nigh** at hand."

So, Luke's statement, "When ye see these things come to pass, know ye that the kingdom of God is nigh at hand", in the context in which it is found, means simply that Jesus was to come near to them in judgement.[12]

This Generation

At Matthew 24:34 having given them the parable of the fig tree, Jesus then says, "Verily I say unto you, This generation (Gk. *genea*[13]) shall not pass, till all these things be fulfilled." How these words have been twisted and tortured in attempts to explain them away! The plain meaning of the words is that all that had been spoken by Jesus in the Olivet Prophecy would be fulfilled in the lifetime of the generation then living. This verse alone demands that the Olivet Prophecy be expounded with reference to AD 70.

---

12. John Thomas writes, "The kingdom of God [was] nigh at hand, when the king, though invisible, was supervising the operation of the siege of his rebellious capital" ("The Prophecy of Mount Olivet", *Herald of the Kingdom and Age to Come*, vol. 3, page 32). For a useful discussion on the "the kingdom of God is nigh" see E. Humphreys, "The Mount Olivet Prophecy", *Testimony*, vol. 47, page 130.

13. "In the New Testament γενεά *[geneá]* is common in the synoptics, rare in Paul, absent from John including the Revelation. It mostly denotes ***generation*** in the sense of contemporaries." (G. Friedrich and G. Kittel, *Theological Dictionary of the New Testament*, vol. 1, page 663.)

"This generation", in the context in which it occurs, cannot refer to a generation many centuries on in time, nor does it relate to a particular race of people,[14] as though Jesus said that the Jewish people would not pass [away] until all had been fulfilled.[15]

The phrase "this generation" in the gospels **always** relates to the generation contemporary with the speaker. Observe how the phrase is used:

> "Whereunto shall I liken **this generation**?" (Matt. 11:16)
>
> "An evil and adulterous **generation** seeketh after a sign... The men of Nineveh shall rise in judgement with **this generation,** and shall condemn it." (Matt. 12:39,41 and see v. 42)
>
> "All these things shall come upon **this generation**" (Matt. 23:36).
>
> "The last state of that man is worse than the first. Even so shall it be also unto **this wicked generation.**" (Matt. 12:45)
>
> "Why doth **this generation** seek after a sign? verily I say unto you, There shall no sign be given unto **this generation.**" (Mark 8:12)

---

14. An example of this view is the following: "Literally, Jesus says, This ***nation***, represented by the fig tree, shall never cease until all these things be fulfilled. The word translated ***generation*** is the word ***geneá*** in the original Greek, and denotes a people or nation. We may, therefore, read Jesus' words as follows — This people or nation shall never pass (perish) till all these things be fulfilled." (M. R. DeHaan, *The Jew and Palestine in Prophecy*, page 151). In connection with DeHaan's biased interpretation of *geneá* see footnote 13 above.

15. The word "pass" in the sentence "this generation shall not ***pass***..." is a translation of *parérchomai,* which means, at this place, "to pass away, perish" (G. Abbott-Smith, *Manual Greek Lexicon*, page 345). Those (e.g. DeHaan, quoted above, and H. Alford in *The New Testament for English Readers*, vol. 1, page 169) who would press this argument, i.e. that "this generation" = the Jewish race, create an insuperable problem. Jesus said, "This generation shall not pass, till all these things be fulfilled." Logically, this must imply that the generation ***will pass*** after the things of which he spoke have been fulfilled. But the purpose of God is centred on the continuing existence of the nation of Israel. Jesus is to reign over the house of Jacob for ever (Luke 1:33). Therefore the ***race*** of Israel will not pass away, or perish, when Jesus returns. Which means that "this generation" which, by implication, Jesus said would pass, cannot refer to the Jewish ***race***. The hypothesis is thus seen to contain its own refutation.

Robert Roberts commented on this very point: " 'This generation shall not pass till all be fulfilled' has reference to the people alive when Christ spoke, and not to the Jewish race or nation, which will never pass." ("Was Redemption Nigh in the Apostolic Age?", *The Christadelphian*, vol. 14, page 378).

> "Whosoever therefore shall be ashamed of me and of my words in **this adulterous and sinful generation;** of him also shall the Son of man be ashamed..." (Mark 8:38)
>
> "**This generation** is an evil generation: it seeketh after a sign; and there shall no sign be given to it but the sign of Jonah. For even as Jonah became a sign unto the Ninevites, so shall also the Son of man be to **this generation.**" (Luke 11:29,30 RV)
>
> "But first must he suffer many things, and be rejected of **this generation.**" (Luke 17:25)

In none of these references can "this generation" mean anything other than the generation contemporary with Jesus and the disciples. One writer, commenting on Matthew 24:34, observes:

> "If dogmatic considerations were not at stake, [this] conclusion would not be questioned, but Biblical exegesis must control Biblical theology, not vice versa. The close parallel to this verse in Mt. 23:36 for most will remove doubts as to the meaning of generation [*genea*] here; it signifies the Jews living in the same age as Jesus." [16, 17]

Anyone coming to the Olivet Prophecy for the first time, with a mind unfettered by preconceived ideas with respect to its interpretation, would understand Jesus to be saying that his own contemporaries would live to see the events that he had predicted.[18]

---

16. G. R. Beasley-Murray, *Jesus and the Future*, page 260.

17. So, John Thomas: "The phrase 'this generation'... refers only to the then existing generation contemporary with Jesus which did not pass till the things predicted of the Desolation were all accomplished." ("Prophecy of Mount Olivet", *Herald of the Kingdom and Age to Come*, vol. 10, page 277.) Also, Robert Roberts: "The generation that heard the words of Christ did not pass away till the predicted destruction of the temple, city, land and people of Israel was accomplished." ("Three Alleged Failures in the Prophecies of Christ", *The Christadelphian*, vol. 35, page 111). So, too, C. C. Walker: "***This generation*** simply means the generation then living. Any other construction does violence to the subject." ("This Generation", *The Christadelphian*, vol. 54, page 358).

18. "What critical torture has been applied to these words to extort from them some other meaning than their obvious and natural one. How has γενεά been hunted through all its lineage and genealogy to discover that it may not mean the persons then living on the earth! But all such efforts are wholly futile. While the words remain in the text their plain and obvious sense will prevail over the glosses and perversions of ingenious criticism." (J. Stuart Russell, *The Parousia*, page 545.)

CHAPTER NINE

WATCH YE THEREFORE

Matthew 24

35 Heaven and earth shall pass away, but my words shall not pass away. 36 But of that day and hour knoweth no man, no, not the angels of heaven, but my father only. 37 But as the days of Noe were, so shall also the coming of the Son of man be. 38 For as in the days that were before the flood they were eating and drinking, marrying and giving in marriage, until the day that Noe entered into the ark, 39 And knew not until the flood came, and took them all away; so shall also the coming of the Son of man be. 40 Then shall two be in the field; the one shall be taken, and the other left. 41 Two women shall be grinding at the mill; the one shall be taken, and the other left. 42 Watch therefore: for ye know not what hour your Lord doth come.

Mark 13

31 Heaven and earth shall pass away: but my words shall not pass away. 32 But of that day and that hour knoweth no man, no, not the angels which are in heaven, neither the Son, but the Father. 33 Take ye heed, watch and pray: for ye know not when the time is. 34 For the Son of man is as a man taking a far journey, who left his house, and gave authority to his servants, and to every man his work, and commanded the porter to watch. 35 Watch ye therefore: for ye know not when the master of the house cometh, at even, or at midnight, or at the cock-crowing, or in the morning: 36 Lest coming suddenly he find you sleeping. 37 And what I say unto you I say unto all, Watch.

Luke 21

33 Heaven and earth shall pass away: but my words shall not pass away 34 And take heed to yourselves, lest at any time your hearts be overcharged with surfeiting, and drunkenness, and cares of this life, and so that day come upon you unawares. 35 For as a snare shall it come on all them that dwell on the face of the whole earth. 36 Watch ye therefore, and pray always, that ye may be accounted worthy to escape all these things that shall come to pass, and to stand before the Son of man.

"Heaven and earth shall pass away" (Matt. 24:35)[1] — so Jesus summarised the devastation that would overtake the nation of Israel. Israel politically organised, with its heavens and its earth—its rulers and its ruled—would be destroyed. The precise time

---

[1] In these words we find a remarkable confirmation of the exposition so far set out. Jesus would appear to be alluding to Psalm 102:25,26 — "Of old hast thou laid the foundation of the earth: and the heavens are the work of thy hands. ***They shall perish,*** but thou shalt endure: yea, all of them shall wax old like a garment ..." The Apostle, in Hebrews 1:10–12 uses these words to demonstrate the superiority of the New Covenant in Christ over the Law Covenant which, as he later shows, at that very time "decayeth and waxeth old [and] is ready to vanish away" (Heb. 8:13 and see comments on page 66-67).

when Israel's commonwealth would be destroyed was, at the time when Jesus spoke these words, known only to the Father (v.36). However, Jesus had given to his disciples the signs that would herald that time of judgement when the city and temple would be reduced to ruins and the nation overthrown. Now, in the remaining verses of the chapter, he gives to them an urgent message of warning and encouragement. He exhorts them to watch patiently for the signs of the approaching time of judgement — "Watch therefore: for ye know not what hour your Lord doth come" (Matt. 24:42).

The Days of Noah

He bases this exhortation to watchfulness upon the experience of those who lived in the days of Noah. The words need to be noted very carefully:

> "As the days of Noe were, so shall also the coming of the Son of man be. For as in the days that were before the flood they were eating and drinking, marrying and giving in marriage, until the day that Noe entered into the ark, And knew not until the flood came, and took them all away; so shall also the coming of the Son of man be. Then shall two be in the field; the one shall be taken, and the other left. Two women shall be grinding at the mill; the one shall be taken, and the other left." (Matt. 24:37–41)

Here, more then anywhere else in the Olivet Prophecy there is a tendency to read into the scriptures preconceived ideas. It is usual to view these verses as saying that at the time of Jesus' still future return, mankind will exhibit violence and immorality similar to that which existed in Noah's day. The living believers will then be snatched away from the midst of a degenerate world and taken to the judgement seat.[2]

---

[2] E.g. "The Lord gave a series of dramatic snapshots of the actual removal of his saints from their normal routine: a woman is snatched away from grinding corn, a man disappears from ploughing…" (H. A. Whittaker, *Studies in the Gospels*, page 614). "The idea of literally travelling through the sky to the judgement seat was plainly taught by our Lord in his explanation of how 'one shall be taken (literally disappear) and another left' at his coming; 'Wheresoever the body is, thither will the eagles be gathered together' (Luke 17:36,37). The point of this allusion is to show that as the eagle travels through the air with a natural homing instinct, without fear or worry as to correct direction, so there should be no

[Footnote continued on next page]

However, read in their context, it is clear that these verses do not have reference to the future coming of Jesus, but that they were fulfilled in the events of AD 70. The reasons for saying this are as follows:

1. As the days of Noe were...

The judgement spoken of was to be the same kind of judgement as that in Noah's days. In the similar section in Luke 17:28,30 the Lord adds a reference to the judgement of Sodom — "As it was in the days of Lot... Even thus shall it be in the day when the Son of man is revealed." In both of these the judgement of God fell upon an apostate people, and faithful people were saved and allowed to continue their ***mortal*** existence. This was true of the vindication of the faithful in AD 70; it will not be so at the Lord's future coming.

2. The epistles show that it was so

It is important to note that it is an **ecclesial** situation that Jesus has in mind. The exhortation to watchfulness was directed to the disciples, for it was the "sons of God" in Noah's day who corrupted God's way and brought judgement upon themselves. Peter, writing to brethren in the Jewish *diaspora* took up the theme of the Olivet Prophecy, and warned of this preoccupation with eating, drinking and marrying when he wrote, "There shall come in the last days[3] scoffers, **walking after their own lusts**, and saying, Where is the promise of his coming?" He, too, then proceeded to compare those last days with the days of Noah (2 Peter 3:3–7).

> "Knowing this first, that there shall come in the last days scoffers, walking after their own lusts, And saying, Where is the promise of his coming? for since the fathers fell asleep, all things continue as they were from the beginning of the creation. For this they willingly are ignorant of, that by the word of God the heavens were of old, and the earth standing out of the water and in the water: Whereby the world that then was, being overflowed

---

apprehension in the mind of the believer concerning the mechanics of how he will be taken away to meet the Lord" (D. Heaster, *The Last Days*, page 224).

[3] I.e. the last days of Israel under the Mosaic system — see pages 16–18 especially footnote 19.

> with water, perished: But the heavens and the earth, which are now, by the same word are kept in store, reserved unto fire against the day of judgment and perdition of ungodly men. (2 Peter 3:3-7)

There can be no doubt that these conditions did come to prevail in the Jewish ecclesias exactly as predicted by Jesus and Peter. Jude later wrote of those who, in his day, were guilty of "turning the grace of our God into lasciviousness" (v.4), who had "gone in the way of Cain" (v.11), and who were "spots in your feasts of charity (i.e. the breaking of bread)" (v.12). He proceeded by quoting Peter's words and applying them to those who, at that time, had been unfaithful to their calling. "These are murmurers, complainers, **walking after their own lusts...** remember ye the words which were spoken before of the apostles of our Lord Jesus Christ; How that they told you there should be **mockers** (Gk. *empaíktēs* = the word rendered "scoffers" in 2 Peter 3:3) **in the last time**, who should **walk after their own ungodly lusts**. These be they..." (Jude vv. 16–19).

Thus the words of Jesus were fulfilled in the experience of the early ecclesia in the "last time", i.e. the period leading up to AD 70. Those days were characterised by a departure from the Truth when the "sons of God" became preoccupied with satisfying their own lusts, so that the days of judgement came upon them unawares. As it was in Noah's day, so it was when judgement fell on ungodly Israel in AD 70.

3. The one shall be taken

Note carefully the record does not say, as is frequently read into the passage, that the faithful will be taken to a place of safety.[4] What it says is:

---

4. There is a worrying emphasis in the writings of those who maintain that the ones "taken" are in fact taken to meet Christ, in that it is only ***the faithful*** who are held to be removed. Thus we have: "...is not 'Taken where?' a needless question, its answer being, fairly obviously: 'Taken to meet their Messiah, of course.' But, 'What shall be the fate of those left behind?' is a natural enough question. And to this Jesus gave answer: 'Those who are spiritually dead will be left to the godless influences where they feel more at home'." (H. A. Whittaker, *Studies in the Gospels*, page 609.) Again: "Those ***wise virgins*** who go forth to

[Footnote continued on next page]

(a) In Noah's day "the **flood** came and **took** them" – i.e. took **the unfaithful!**

(b) So too at the coming of the Son of man "one shall be **taken** ..."

On a number of occasions (e.g. pages 10, 27, 58–59, 80–81) we have seen the parallel between the Babylonian invasion in the time of Jeremiah, and the Roman invasion predicted by the Lord in the Olivet Prophecy. It is therefore interesting to see that, in connection with the Babylonian invasion, two groups of people are referred to in these same terms:

> "But the Chaldeans' army pursued after them, and overtook Zedekiah in the plains of Jericho: and when they had **taken** him, they brought him up to Nebuchadnezzar king of Babylon to Riblah in the land of Hamath, where he gave judgment upon him... But Nebuzaradan the captain of the guard **left** of the poor of the people, which had nothing, in the land of Judah, and gave them vineyards and fields at the same time." (Jer. 39:5,10)

Thus, Zedekiah that "profane wicked prince of Israel", with his companions, are said to have been "**taken**" (Jer. 39:5), whilst the oppressed poor in Israel were "**left**... in the land" (v. 10).

Those who are "taken" are the ones who suffer in the judgements. Those who are "left" are those who are spared. The words used in the gospel confirm this. The word "taken" (Gk. *paralambánō*) means to 'take away', not to 'save or deliver'.[5] The word "left"

---

meet Christ immediately are therefore those who will be 'caught up together' with the ***faithful*** believers who will have been resurrected." (D. Heaster, *The Last Days*, page 223.) Although those who argue thus would firmly maintain a belief in the reality of "the judgement seat of Christ" yet of necessity they have to argue for two separate 'takings away' — one of the faithful, who are taken out of trouble, and one of the unfaithful which takes place later. This appears to have serious implications, not least of which is that if there has been separation into two groups then it would appear that judgement has already taken place.

5. "*PARALAMBANŌ* (παραλαμβάνω)... denotes to take to (or with) oneself... [and is used] of the removal of persons from the earth in judgement" (W. E. Vine, *Expository Dictionary of New Testament Words*, vol. 4, page 105). "*PARALAMBANŌ* — to take to oneself, seize or take into one's possession... In Matt. 24:40,41; Lk. 17:34,35 *paralambánō* in the passive form is used as the opposite of *aphíēmi*, to let be. In these verses, those who are taken are not to be

[Footnote continued on next page]

(Gk. *aphíēmi*) does not mean 'left behind', but 'spared or saved'.[6] That this is the right way to look at this is confirmed by the Lord's words in Luke 21:34, 35, which must now be examined.

Take Heed to Yourselves

In Luke's account Jesus continues the exhortation to his disciples saying, "And take heed to yourselves, lest at any time your hearts be overcharged with surfeiting, and drunkenness, and cares of this life, and so that day come upon you unawares. For as a snare shall it come on all them that dwell on the face of the whole earth" (Luke 21:34, 35).

The word "earth" here is a translation of the Greek word *gē*,[7] and refers to the land of Israel. For the Jews in the land, the coming of the Son of man would be as a snare. The believers were to take heed to themselves, lest they also were overtaken unawares by the coming calamities.

The reference to "a snare" is interesting. Jesus appears to be alluding again[8] to Isaiah chapter 8:

> "Sanctify the LORD of hosts himself: and let him be your fear, and let him be your dread. And he shall be for a sanctuary; but for a stone of stumbling and for a rock of offence to both the houses of Israel, for a gin and for **a snare** to the inhabitants of Jerusalem." (vv.13,14)

---

misconstrued as those whom the Lord favours..." (S. Zodhiates, *The Complete Word Study Dictionary: New Testament*, page 1108).

6. "*APHIĒMI* (ἀφίημι)...has the chief meanings: (a) to send forth, to let go, forgive, (b) to let, suffer [i.e. to allow], permit (c) to leave, leave alone, forsake, neglect." (W. E. Vine, *Expository Dictionary of New Testament Words*, vol. 2, page 325). "*Aphiēmi* — To let go from one's power or possession, to go free, let escape. (Matt. 24:40,41; Lk. 17:34–35; LXX Prov. 4:13)." (S. Zodhiates, *The Complete Word Study Dictionary: New Testament*, page 299).

7. "*GĒ* (γῆ), in one of its usages, denotes (a) land as distinct from sea... (b) land as subject to cultivation... (c) land as describing a country or region..." (W. E. Vine, *Expository Dictionary of New Testament Words*, vol. 2, page 308). S. Zodhiates gives as one of the meanings of *gē*, "A country, region, territory, as the land of Israel... Spoken particularly of and used in an absolute sense of the land of the Jews, Palestine..." (*The Complete Word Study Dictionary: New Testament*, page 367).

8. See footnote 17, page 15.

The Jews stumbled at the stumbling stone when they crucified Jesus, as Paul in Romans 9:32 makes clear. Isaiah spoke further of this stumbling when he predicted: "And many among them shall **stumble"**; to which he added, "and fall, and be broken, and be **snared**, and be **taken**" (v.15). This is what happened in AD 70. The events overtook them in the way that an animal is unexpectedly trapped in a snare. They were also **broken**. The stone which the Jews stumbled over became the instrument of their own destruction, as foretold by Jesus himself: "Whosoever shall fall upon that stone shall be **broken**; but on whomsoever it shall fall, it will grind him to powder" (Luke 20:18). And, as we have seen, they were also **taken**. In the days of Noah, the flood came, and the wicked were taken away. So also would the coming of the Son of man be. Two men would be in the field, the wicked man would be **taken**, and the righteous left, or spared.

How were the disciples to escape such things? By diligent and prayerful watching of the signs of the times. Jesus therefore exhorts his disciples: "**Watch** ye therefore, and **pray always**, that ye may be accounted worthy to escape all these things that shall come to pass, and to stand before the Son of man"[9] (Luke 21:36). This was not the first time that Jesus emphasised the importance of prayer for those who wished to escape the holocaust of those

---

9. Some may find difficulty in using the phrase "to stand before the Son of man" of the disciples who were afforded deliverance from the AD 70 judgements. However, it cannot be denied that, in the context, standing before the Son of man is the consequence of escaping those things that were to overtake the inhabitants of the land as a snare. The same word is used of the Ephesians who were called upon to fight "against principalities, against powers, against the rulers of the darkness of this world, against spiritual wickedness in high places" as they sought to remain faithful in the Gentile world. To this end they were exhorted to "Take unto you the whole armour of God, that ye may be able to withstand in the evil day, and having done all, to ***stand***. ***Stand*** therefore, having your loins girt about with truth..." (Eph. 6:12–14). Thus, "standing before the Son of man" implies being shown to be faithful to him in the face of very difficult circumstances. The events of the sixth seal have many parallels with the Olivet Prophecy and of these events it is said, "The great day of his wrath is come; and who shall be able to ***stand***?" (Rev. 6:17). In the outpouring of God's wrath in AD 70 the answer to this searching question is — Those who faithfully obeyed the words of the Son of man.

days. Earlier in the Olivet Prophecy Jesus said, "But pray ye that your flight be not in the winter, neither on the sabbath day" (Matt. 24:20). Similarly, the reason for giving the parable of the unjust judge to his disciples was that, in the troubles leading up to the AD 70 judgements, "men ought **always to pray**, and not to faint" (Luke 18:1).

CHAPTER TEN

THE GOOD AND EVIL SERVANTS

Matthew 24

43 But know this, that if the goodman of the
house had known in what watch the thief
would come, he would have watched, and
would not have suffered his house to be
broken up. 44 Therefore be ye also ready: for
in such an hour as ye think not the Son of
man cometh. 45 Who then is a faithful and
wise servant, whom his lord hath made ruler
over his household, to give them meat in due
season? 46 Blessed is that servant, whom
his lord when he cometh shall find so doing.
47 Verily I say unto you, That he shall make
him ruler over all his goods. 48 But and if that
evil servant shall say in his heart, My lord
delayeth his coming; 49 And shall begin to
smite his fellowservants, and to eat and drink
with the drunken; 50 The lord of that servant
shall come in a day when he looketh not for
him, and in an hour that he is not aware of,
51 And shall cut him asunder, and appoint
him his portion with the hypocrites: there
shall be weeping and gnashing of teeth.

As a Thief

The day of destruction was to come suddenly — as a snare — to all that dwelt in the land of Israel. Jesus now further compares his coming in judgement against Israel to the coming of a thief. Obviously, if the master of the house had known beforehand that a robbery was planned, he would have taken precautions. The coming of Jesus would be sudden and unexpected as far as the nation as a whole was concerned, but his followers should have been ready. Sadly, it would appear that many of them were not. They lightly regarded his words of warning and failed to flee from Judaea when they saw the Roman abomination of desolation arrive in the land in AD 66. In AD 68 when Vespasian withdrew his forces because of trouble in Rome, hesitant believers were given another opportunity to get out. But when the Roman armies returned and closed their grip on Judaea and Jerusalem the faithless and disobedient were taken by surprise and suffered in the judgement that marked the consummation of that age.

As we have seen previously, 2 Peter ch. 3 is a prophecy about these same judgements and it is not surprising that the apostle there refers back to this teaching of the Lord when he warns those to whom he writes, "The day of the Lord will come **as a thief** in the night; in the which the heavens shall pass away with a great noise…" (2 Pet. 3:10).[1]

The Faithful and Wise Servants

Having warned his disciples that there will be many in Israel who will be totally unprepared for the time of judgement, Jesus now turns to his disciples and gives them a most sober warning. Even among the **servants** in the household there will be those who had listened to his warnings and had disregarded them – there will be both faithful and unfaithful.

Consider first what is said about the faithful servants, for here again is language that ties the prophecy to the AD 70 period. "Who then is a faithful and wise servant, whom his lord hath made ruler over his household, to give them meat in due season?" (Matt. 24:45).

Transferring these ideas to the Lord's own household of which he is clearly speaking, the faithful servant represents that class of believers:

1. That was appointed by the Lord,

---

[1] It is relevant to remind ourselves that Peter continues here, "…and ***the elements*** shall melt with fervent heat…" The Greek word translated 'elements' is *stoicheíon*. The word only occurs seven times in scripture and in every case has reference to the constituent parts of the Law that were to be done away in the conflagration of AD 70. The use of the term in Paul's letter to the Galatians — an ecclesia that was intent on returning to the Law as a means of salvation — will illustrate its usage. "Even so we, when we were children, were in bondage under ***the elements*** of the world… But now, after that ye have known God, or rather are known of God, how turn ye again to the weak and beggarly ***elements,*** whereunto ye desire again to be in bondage? Ye observe days, and months, and times, and years" (Gal. 4:3, 9–10). The use of the word by Peter provides further confirmation that it is correct to expound this prophecy in relation to the termination of the Mosaic arrangement of things. See also comments on pages 70–71.

It is worth noting here that there is absolutely no justification for applying Peter's reference to the elements melting with fervent heat, to the effects of nuclear explosion. If, as some allege, it is the literal elements that are to melt, then it follows that it is the literal heavens that are to pass away with a great noise. Scriptures such as Jer. 31:35–37 show that will not be the case.

2. That constituted rulers in the household, and
3. That provided (spiritual) meat to the household.

This language has reference to a First Century situation. In apostolic times there was a "faithful and wise servant" class of believers to whom the Lord gave special holy spirit gifts, which enabled them to guide the Christian congregations "into all the truth" (John 16:13 RV). This activity of holy spirit was given, said the Lord, To "teach [them] all things" and to "bring all things to [their] remembrance, whatsoever [Jesus had] said unto [them]" (John 14:26). It was also given "to show [them] things to come" (John 16:13). By the exercise of these gifts the apostles, prophets, evangelists, pastors and teachers (Eph. 4:11) were able to supply the household with its necessary "meat in due season." These brethren were rulers in the congregations – "Obey them that have the rule over you" (Heb. 13:17), exhorts the apostle. Today, there are no divinely appointed rulers in the household and none with gifts of holy spirit. The words can only apply to the apostolic age leading up to the time of the Lord's coming in judgement in AD 70.

The Evil Servants

Consideration of what is said about the condition of the evil servants at the time of the Lord's coming, also supports the view that it is the coming in judgement in AD 70 that is being spoken about:

> "If that evil servant shall say in his heart, My Lord delayeth his coming; and shall begin to smite his fellowservants, and to eat and drink with the drunken; the lord of that servant shall come in a day when he looketh not for him, and in an hour that he is not aware of." (Matt. 24:48–50)

The epistles demonstrate that this evil servant-class abounded in the ecclesias around the time of the AD 70 judgements.

Paul wrote of them, describing them as:

> "False apostles, deceitful workers, transforming themselves into the apostles of Christ." (2 Cor. 11:13)

John cautioned the brethren:

> "Beloved, believe not every spirit, but try the spirits whether they are of God: because many false prophets are gone out into the world." (1 John 4:1)

Peter wrote at length concerning them in his second letter and spoke of their wide-spread influence among the Jewish brethren:

> "But there were false prophets also among the people, even as there shall be false teachers among you, who privily shall bring in damnable heresies, even denying the Lord that bought them, and bring upon themselves swift destruction. And many shall follow their pernicious ways; by reason of whom the way of truth shall be evil spoken of." (2 Pet. 2:1–2)

James referred to them when he rebuked the rich:

> "Ye have laid up your treasure in the last days. Behold, the hire of the labourers who mowed your fields, which is of you kept back by fraud, crieth out: and the cries of them that reaped have entered into the ears of the Lord of Sabaoth. Ye have lived delicately on the earth, and taken your pleasure; ye have nourished your hearts in a day of slaughter." (James 5:3–5 RV)

It is of these unfaithful servants that Jude writes:

> "There are certain men crept in unawares... ungodly men, turning the grace of our God into lasciviousness... These are spots in your feasts of charity, when they feast with you, feeding themselves without fear: clouds they are without water, carried about of winds; trees whose fruit withereth, without fruit, twice dead, plucked up by the roots." (vv. 4,12)

Thus the epistles demonstrate that the words of Jesus were fulfilled in apostolic times. There did arise an evil servant-class among the brethren.

With the Hypocrites

But what would happen to them? "The lord of that servant shall come... and appoint him his portion **with the hypocrites**" (Matt. 24:50,51). The definite article is present in the Greek text — "with **the** hypocrites" — i.e. the hypocrites previously spoken of at great length in the temple precincts just before he departed to the Mount of Olives where he delivered the Olivet Prophecy. Following the Revised Version it is recorded that Jesus pronounced seven "woes" upon the scribes and Pharisees, on each occasion calling them "hypocrites" (Matt. 23:13, 15, 16, 23, 25, 27, 29 — verse 14 is omitted in the RV). In his last pronunciation of "Woe unto [the] Scribes and Pharisees, hypocrites," Jesus proceeds to speak of them filling up the measure of their iniquity (by putting him to death). The inevitable consequence of this was: "Upon you [shall] come all the righteous blood shed upon the earth... these things shall come upon **this generation**" (Matt. 23:35–36). Thus the Lord was warning that the evil servants would suffer with the scribes and Pharisees in the events of AD 70.

Detail from the arch of Titus showing Jews being taken into exile with Temple treasures

"The lord of that [evil] servant shall... appoint him his portion with the hypocrites: there shall be weeping and gnashing of teeth."

What About Us?

Not infrequently the response to such exposition as has been set out in these pages is — If the coming of Jesus spoken of in this prophecy applies to his coming in judgement at the close of the Mosaic age then what does it hold for us?[2] However, perhaps it

[2] The most extreme example of the desire to give the words of the Lord on Mount Olivet an application to our own situation is seen in the teaching of those who adopt a futurist approach to the entire prophecy. They maintain that the

[Footnote continued on next page]

would be more appropriate to ask – if the prophecy applies to our days then what did it offer those brethren of the first century to whom it was given? For that matter what has it offered believers during the long centuries from then until now? What right have we to appropriate to ourselves words that the Lord himself clearly said were for the generation to whom his remarks were addressed?

The judgement of God upon Israel in AD 70 was terrible and far-reaching. Israel had filled the cup of her iniquity. The longsuffering of God towards that favoured nation was at last exhausted. The blood of prophets and apostles cried out from the ground. The LORD had visited his people and they had rejected him and crucified the Son of his love through whom he had revealed himself to them. The "days of vengeance" had arrived. The nation was to be dissolved; the Law covenant, rendered obsolete by the death of Jesus, was to be formally taken away; the people were to be scattered, despised and persecuted for centuries to come. Meanwhile a new age had arrived – an age of opportunity for the Gentiles. This is the true significance of the Olivet Prophecy for us – a significance that has had meaning to Gentiles of all the centuries since AD 70.

It should occasion no surprise that the Lord Jesus should give to his disciples, at this critical time in Israel's history, a detailed prophecy in order to prepare their minds for those momentous events that were about to happen in their days.

However, it is incumbent upon us to take from the Lord's message to the believers of those days, instruction and exhortation as we seek to wait faithfully for the end-time coming of the Lord

---

temple must be rebuilt and animal sacrifices resumed. Only then will Israel be overturned by a latter day "abomination of desolation" and the Olivet Prophecy fulfilled. I first heard this view set out from a Christadelphian platform in the 1950s. It appears to have resurfaced recently. E.g. "The entire prophecy is related to the last days, there are no references to AD 70..." (C. Brown, "The Truth About the Olivet Prophecy", *The Way Ahead*, March–April, 2003.) "The Olivet Prophecy is not about AD 70." (Maurice Beale, "Concerning a 'third' Jewish Temple", *Testimony*, vol. 75, page 90.)

Jesus. This we seek to do from all the Scriptures. When Jeremiah prophesied to the unfaithful nation of Israel of the impending judgement of God about to be meted out upon them by the Babylonian armies, he gave repeated exhortation such as:

> "...thus saith the LORD to the men of Judah and Jerusalem, Break up your fallow ground, and sow not among thorns. Circumcise yourselves to the LORD, and take away the foreskins of your heart, ye men of Judah and inhabitants of Jerusalem: lest my fury come forth like fire, and burn that none can quench it, because of the evil of your doings" (Jer. 4:3-4)

In the godless, immoral, materialistic, world of today the Ecclesia is under increasing pressure to conform to the world's perverse ways and there is clear evidence that the battle is being lost in some respects at least. As we see the judgements of God approaching it is proper that we apply the powerful exhortation of Jeremiah to ourselves in our situation — to break up **our** fallow ground, and not to sow among thorns; to circumcise the foreskin of **our** hearts. So we can take exhortation from the words of Jeremiah. However, this does not change the indisputable fact that the prophecy was given to Israel, and applied only to Israel, and was fulfilled exclusively with reference to Israel.

So too with the Olivet Prophecy; it was given to meet the specific circumstances faced by the believers as the AD 70 judgements approached. To take scripture that had specific reference to the AD 70 period and apply it to us betrays a careless use of scripture. But the **lessons** inherent in the Olivet Prophecy are there for us to take to ourselves. The importance of watching the signs of the times; the need to faithfully endure the trying times that lead up to appearing of the Lord Jesus; the need to be faithful in our stewardship as the day approaches — are all timeless lessons that we can apply to ourselves. It is true of the Olivet Prophecy, as of all other scripture, that "whatsoever things were written aforetime were written for our learning, that we through patience and comfort of the scriptures might have hope" (Rom. 15:4). But this does not give us license us to play fast and loose with the Lord's words, or absolve us from the responsibility of seeking to faithfully expound the message in its context.

Dual Application?

Some would accept that the Olivet Prophecy has an application to the events associated with AD 70 but would then argue that the prophecy has what they call 'a dual application'. By this they mean that parts of the prophecy, at least, have another level of meaning and refer to the end-time and events leading up to the second advent. So they maintain the "wars and rumours of wars" (Matt. 24:6), "earthquakes in divers places" (Matt. 24:7), the preaching of the gospel to all nations (Matt. 24:14), the signs in the sun, moon and stars (Matt. 24:29), all truly refer to AD 70 events, but they also refer to events in the Gentile world of our days. There are many problems with this approach but by far the most serious is the fact that a prophecy that is admitted to be about Israel and which was fulfilled with respect to Israel in AD 70, is taken out of its context and applied to the Gentile world. This seems to me to be unjustifiable.

It would be foolish to discount altogether the possibility of a dual application of the Olivet Prophecy. However, in my view those who support a 'dual application' have yet to present a carefully reasoned, scriptural, argument for their cause that is worthy of serious consideration. No good will be done by wresting scriptures out of context and applying them randomly according to whim.

The Future

The Olivet Prophecy does speak of days yet future. Because of chapter headings in our Bibles, the fact that Matthew ch. 25 is part of the Olivet Prophecy is often overlooked. The purpose of this exposition has been to examine the parallel accounts of Matthew 24, Mark 13 and Luke 21. There is nothing in Mark and Luke that corresponds to Matthew 25 and it is not intended to consider this chapter in any detail. However, the point must be made that at Matthew 25:31 there can be no doubt that the Lord speaks of events that are still future. It is the time when "the Son of man shall come in his glory, and all the holy angels with him, [and when he shall] sit upon the throne of his glory". Jesus is to return to take up the position covenanted to him (2 Sam. 7:12–13; Luke 1:30–33), and to reign on David's throne in Jerusalem. At this time "the Son of man" comes not to judge Israel but "before him shall be gathered **all nations**:[3] and he shall separate them one from another, as a shepherd divideth his sheep from the goats" (Matt. 25:32).

For this time all who, during the long period of Israel's downtreading, have been born into Zion's family (Isaiah 54:1,13; Psalm 87:5,6) pray daily. They marvel at the outworking of God's purpose wherein, through Israel's fall, outlined in the Olivet Prophecy, the gospel has trumpeted forth so that "salvation is come unto the Gentiles" (Rom. 11:11). They heed the warning of the great apostle to the Gentiles— "because of unbelief they [Israel] were broken off, and thou standest by faith. Be not highminded, but fear: for if God spared not the natural branches, take heed lest he also spare not thee" (Rom. 11:20, 21). They know that "blindness in part is happened to Israel, **until** the fulness (= full number) of the Gentiles be come in" (Rom. 11:25). With gratitude they live for that time when, "There shall come out of Sion the Deliverer, and shall turn away ungodliness from Jacob" (Rom. 11:26).

---

3. Gk. *éthnos*, here translated "nations", when used in the plural with the article denotes "***the nations***, as distinct from Israel, ***Gentiles***" (G. Abbott-Smith, *Manual Greek Lexicon of the New Testament*, page 129). So it is the still future judgement of the nations that is being presented here.

APPENDIX

REALISED ESCHATOLOGY— IS IT SUSTAINABLE?

What is Realised Eschatology?

Perhaps many readers of this book will not have heard of 'realised eschatology'— sometimes referred to as 'fulfilled eschatology' or 'covenant eschatology'. The word *eschatology* means, simply, a study of the last things. In the evangelical churches, especially in the USA, there has arisen in recent years a growing body of opinion, which, having come to appreciate the force of the argument for the AD 70 fulfilment of the Olivet Prophecy, has built around this the concept of realised eschatology. They maintain that:

> "The holy scriptures teach that the second coming of Christ, including the establishment of the eternal kingdom, the day of judgement, the end of the world and the resurrection of the dead, occurred with the fall of Jerusalem in AD 70."[1]

There are some variations in detail but this definition is generally applicable.

In their writings, the realised eschatologists correctly identify "the end of the world" (the consummation of the age) in Matthew 24:3 as the dissolution of Israel's commonwealth. They also, correctly, see the coming of the Roman armies to bring about this end of the Mosaic arrangement of things as a "coming" of Jesus in the sense set out in this study. He came against Israel through the agency of the Roman armies in the same way that Jehovah came against them in the Babylonian armies in Old Testament times. Their arguments in this respect are, for the most part, scriptural and carefully reasoned.[2]

---

1. A statement of the realised eschatology position quoted by Olan Hicks, *The AD 70 Theory*, page 5.

2. One of the most carefully reasoned works in this respect is *Matthew 24 Fulfilled*, by John L. Bray, originally published as a series of booklets 1990–1996.

However, because of other theological concepts that cannot be substantiated from scripture, most realised eschatologists are able to argue that this coming of Jesus against Jerusalem is the only coming of Jesus mentioned in the Bible; that the resurrection and judgement have already taken place; and that Jesus is even now reigning in his kingdom. The proponents of this theory, for the most part, appear to reach their conclusions by a system of extremely convoluted and complicated reasoning which refuses to take scripture at its face value, forcing upon it an interpretation that is unsustainable. They do to other scriptures what they accuse others of doing with respect to the Olivet Prophecy.

The Fundamental Problem

Before examining briefly some of the tenets of realised eschatology it will be as well to point out the reason why its proponents are so easily able to dismiss the clear teaching of a future resurrection and judgement and why, in spite of the obvious chaos present in the world, they are able to believe that Christ is already reigning in his kingdom.

They do not believe that Christ's kingdom is yet to be established on the earth. They maintain that Christ is now reigning from heaven and that people are taken to heaven as each one dies. Thus the promise to the apostles that "in the regeneration when the Son of man shall sit in the throne of his glory, ye also shall sit upon twelve thrones, judging the twelve tribes of Israel" (Matt. 19:28), is taken to mean that in AD 70 the apostles were in heaven supervising the judgement of God upon Israel![3] In short they subscribe to the pagan concept of the immortality of the soul which has no basis in scripture and is so destructive of revealed truth. In this connection, the following brief comments are offered:

1. There is not a single verse in scripture that states in unequivocal terms that man has an immortal soul that goes to heaven (or to any other place) at death. The Bible teaches that

---

3. *Bible Prophecy*, John L. Bray, page 82.

man is mortal and that when he dies he is really dead. For example:

"And unto Adam he said, Because thou hast hearkened unto the voice of thy wife, and hast eaten of the tree, of which I commanded thee, saying, Thou shalt not eat of it: cursed is the ground for thy sake; in sorrow shalt thou eat of it all the days of thy life; Thorns also and thistles shall it bring forth to thee; and thou shalt eat the herb of the field; In the sweat of thy face shalt thou eat bread, till thou **return unto the ground**; for out of it wast thou taken: for **dust thou art, and unto dust shalt thou return**." (Gen. 3:17–19)

"For as **in Adam all die**, even so in Christ shall all be made alive." (1 Cor. 15:22)

"For **in death there is no remembrance of thee**: in the grave who shall give thee thanks?" (Psalm 6:5)

"For the living know that they shall die: but **the dead know not any thing**, neither have they any more a reward; for the memory of them is forgotten. Also their **love, and their hatred, and their envy, is now perished**; neither have they any more a portion for ever in any thing that is done under the sun ... Whatsoever thy hand findeth to do, do it with thy might; for **there is no work, nor device, nor knowledge, nor wisdom, in the grave**, whither thou goest." (Eccl. 9:5,6,10)

To return to the dust and to oblivion is the lot of all mankind apart from the sacrifice of Jesus. It is only by an association with him and his sacrifice that men can be brought into a relationship with eternal life. So we read, "But **as many** as received him, to them gave he power to become the sons of God, even to them that believe on his name" (John 1:12). Apart from this association with Jesus, men are said to 'perish'—"God so loved the world, that he gave his only begotten Son, that **whosoever** believeth in him should not perish, but have everlasting life" (John 3:16). Thus, those who do not believe (Gk. *pisteúō* = 'have faith') will perish. Of these the apostle speaks when he says that the Gentiles not related to Christ's sacrifice, "walk in the vanity of their mind, having the understanding darkened, being **alienated from the life of God** through the ignorance that is in them..." (Eph. 4:17, 18).

2. The doctrine of the immortality of the soul is not scriptural. It is pagan in origin as has been admitted by honest orthodox churchmen and commentators as the following quotations illustrate:

> "The idea of the inherent indestructibility of the human soul (or consciousness) owes its origin to Greek, not to Bible, sources." (*Towards the Conversion of England — A Report of a Commission on Evangelism Appointed by the Archbishops of Canterbury and York*, page 23)
>
> "The Bible knows nothing either of the expression *the immortality of the soul*, or of the modern doctrine as to immortality." (H. Olshausen, *Commentary on the Gospels*, vol. 3, page 67)
>
> "Plato taught that the soul of man is immortal and imperishable... In this respect, modern popular Christian eschatology is much nearer to Plato than to Christ... the doctrine of the immortality of the soul... has no place in the teaching of Christ and his Apostles." (*The Immortality of the Soul*, J. Agar-Beet, pages 34–36).

3. Adherence to the idea that there is a part of our being that continues to live when the body dies makes it easy for realised eschatology to modify the clear Bible teaching of the second coming, the resurrection, and judgement. Since the hope for the future is to go to heaven to be with Jesus, there is really little point in him coming back to the earth. Similarly with respect to resurrection and judgement. If, when a person dies, he proceeds to heaven, then judgement has already taken place, he has received his reward and there is little point in bodily resurrection and subsequent judgement.

Thus, since the adherents of fulfilled eschatology hold fast to this pagan teaching (or thinly disguised modifications of it) with respect to the afterlife, it is not surprising that they are unable to rightly divide the Word with respect to "the last things".

The New Covenant

Central to the 'last things' is the 'new covenant'. It seems to me that realised eschatology misunderstands the new covenant and its relationship to the old covenant.

The old covenant was the Mosaic Law covenant which was a temporary arrangement introduced into the national life of Israel to act as a "schoolmaster" (Gal. 3:24) to look over the nation until the appearing of Messiah in their midst. The need for the schoolmaster is evident from a consideration of the early history of the divinely chosen nation. Left to themselves they would have completely apostatised with the surrounding pagan peoples (e.g.

see Num. 25; Jud. 2:17; Jer. 3:2; etc.). The intermarriage and apostasy of the nation would have meant that the "holy seed" would have become mingled with the pagan Gentiles so that the promised seed of Abraham (Gen. 22:17, 18) through the tribe of Judah (Gen. 49:10) and the house of David (2 Sam. 7:12–14) could not have materialised. So says the apostle, "It (i.e. the Law covenant) was added because of transgressions, till the seed should come to whom the promise was made…" (Gal. 3:19). Its statutes helped to keep them separate from the Gentiles.

Thus the Law was never intended to be a means of individual salvation. Salvation at all times in history since the Fall has been offered to men on the basis of faith. So we are told that, "Abraham believed [Gk. *epísteusen* = lit. 'faithed'] God, and it was counted unto him for righteousness [Gk. *dikaiosúnen* = 'justification']" (Rom. 4:3). In other words Abraham was "justified by faith". The things believed (i.e. 'faithed') by Abraham were the things that God had promised. The things promised were centred on a "seed" who would "possess the gate of his enemies" and through whom "all the nations of the earth [would] be blessed" (Gen. 22:17, 18). The "blessing" of all nations here envisaged was, in the first place, the offer of forgiveness to those showing faith (Acts 3:26; Gal. 3:8). This promise of a "seed" who would bring salvation was a development of the promise in Eden of a "seed" who would destroy the serpent (Gen. 3:15). The promise was further elaborated to David who also was promised a "seed" who, being Son of God and Son of man, would in his suffering for iniquity[4] be

---

4. The words of the AV here are, "If he commit iniquity, I will chasten him with the rod of men…" etc. The words "commit iniquity" are from the Hebrew word *avah,* which signifies "to bend, to curve, to twist, to distort" (Gesenius, *Hebrew and Chaldee Lexicon*, page 611). In this verse it refers to Messiah's being bent because of the weight of that which he carried — "Surely he hath borne our griefs and carried our sorrows". Adam Clarke thus captures the sense in his *Bible Commentary* when he renders it, "In his suffering for iniquity I will chasten him with the rod of men…" John Thomas conveys the sense beautifully when he translates it — "Who in his being caused to bow down, I will chasten him..." ("Promises Covenanted To David", *Herald of the Kingdom and Age to Come*, vol. 8, page 172).

chastened "with the rod of men, and with the stripes of the children of men" (2 Sam. 7:14; cf. Isa. 53:4, 5). David refers to this promise as "an everlasting covenant" (2 Sam. 23:5; see also Isa. 55:3 and note how Paul, in Acts 13:34, associates the victorious resurrection of Jesus with this "everlasting covenant, even the sure mercies of David").

These promises so carefully set out in the Old Testament scriptures were in fact the terms of the new covenant which was ratified by the shedding of the blood of Jesus (Heb. 9:15–17) so that, in consequence of his death and resurrection, "all the promises of God in him are yea, and in him Amen (i.e. sure)..." (2 Cor. 1:20). Thus the death of Jesus at one and the same time removed the Law covenant (Col. 2:14) and ratified the "everlasting covenant" promises that actually **predated** the Law covenant (Gal. 3:17). These promises are styled by the apostle, "The covenant, that was confirmed before of God in Christ", which the Law covenant did not in any way disannul.

Whilst it is conceded that the events of AD 70 removed the trappings of the temporary Law covenant – the Temple, the sacrificial ritual etc. – Christ had already removed from his Jewish followers any obligation to observe the Law (e.g. see Gal. 2:11–21; Gal. 4). AD 70 cannot in any way be considered to be the beginning of the new covenant. The terms of the covenant were set out clearly in Old Testament times and were ratified by the sacrifice of Jesus. AD 70 was irrelevant to that ratification.

The Kingdom of God

The subject of the Kingdom of God cannot be separated from the new covenant. The realised eschatology position is that all the promises of God with respect to Israel and Christ's kingdom received their fulfilment in AD 70. So we are told:

> "Christ was preached consistently as the fulfilment of the law, the prophets and psalms, a work that extended to his age-consummating parousia within

> the same generation of his death and resurrection. Nothing failed to come to pass. No promise was left unfulfilled."[5]

Such statements show a lamentable lack of appreciation of the Old Testament prophets that were endorsed by the Lord and his apostles.

For example, we have already made brief reference to the covenant that God made with David in 2 Samuel 7:12–16:

> "12 And when thy days be fulfilled, and thou shalt sleep with thy fathers, I will set up thy seed after thee, which shall proceed out of thy bowels, and I will establish his kingdom. 13 He shall build an house for my name, and I will stablish the throne of his kingdom for ever. 14 I will be his father, and he shall be my son. If he commit iniquity, I will chasten him with the rod of men, and with the stripes of the children of men: 15 But my mercy shall not depart away from him, as I took it from Saul, whom I put away before thee. 16 And thine house and thy kingdom shall be established for ever before thee: thy throne shall be established for ever."

This promise, in very simple and easy to be understood words, says that at some date future to his death (referred to as sleeping with his fathers) David would have a descendant of whom it is said that:

1. He would build a house (or family) for God's name (v. 13).
2. God would be his Father (v. 14).
3. He would suffer for iniquity[6] being chastened with the rod of men and the stripes of the children of men (v. 14, cf. Isaiah 53:5).
4. God would establish the throne of his kingdom for ever—which is elaborated as David's kingdom being established for ever (vv. 13, 16).
5. Although these things were to happen after David had died, David would be there to see it—"Thine house and thy kingdom shall be established for ever before thee" (v. 16).

---

5. M. King, *The Cross and the Parousia of Christ*, page 381.
6. See footnote 4, page 124.

That this prophecy concerns the work of the Lord Jesus, there can be no doubt. He is introduced in the first verse of the New Testament as "Jesus Christ, **the Son of David**..." The promise that he is to reign on David's throne for ever was reaffirmed by the angel to Mary – "He shall be great, and shall be called the Son of the Highest: and the Lord God shall give unto him the throne of his father David: And he shall reign over the house of Jacob for ever; and of his kingdom there shall be no end" (Luke 1:32, 33). 2 Samuel 7:14 is expressly quoted by the apostle in Hebrews 1:5 as referring to the Lord Jesus. The New Testament makes it plain:

1. That Jesus was born Son of David and Son of God (Matt. 1:1, 20; Luke 1:32).
2. That he did suffer for iniquity and was, in this suffering, chastened with the rod of men and with the stripes of the children of men (e.g. 1 Peter 2:24).
3. That by his death and resurrection he commenced the work of building a house (family) for God's name. Paul writes that he was highly exalted and given "**the name** which is above every name" (Phil. 2:9 RV). Given the Name he became the firstborn of the Divine family (Col. 1:18; Heb. 2:10; Rom. 1:4), the chief corner stone in the foundation of God's house (1 Pet. 2:6–7; Eph. 2:20).

All these things were fulfilled in reality and we can understand them without having to perform mental gymnastics. The words of the promise meant exactly what they said. But there is not one shred of evidence that supports the view that the wording of the other terms of the covenant must be interpreted before they can be understood. Jesus has not yet established David's kingdom; he is not yet reigning on David's throne. The only way in which it can be maintained that these aspects of the covenant prophecy have already been fulfilled, is to give the words a meaning that they do not contain.[7]

---

7. So King writes concerning the scriptures that promise that Jesus would reign on David's throne — "These scriptures, in their description of Christ's reign, are

[Footnote continued on next page]

Israel

If all God's promises were fulfilled in AD 70 then clearly Israel has no further part to play in God's purpose. So we are told – "When Jerusalem was destroyed... every prophecy in the Bible that ever had anything to do with Israel was now fulfilled."[8]

The statement of the angel to Mary was quite clear. "He shall be great, and shall be called the Son of the Highest: and the Lord God shall give unto him the throne of his father David: and he shall reign over the house of Jacob for ever; and of his kingdom there shall be no end" (Luke 1:32, 33). David reigned over the people of Israel, otherwise known as the house of Jacob. If words mean anything this promise can only mean that Jesus is to reign over that same people. It is clear that realised eschatologists, although I believe most of them to be sincere and honest, have a problem. They believe that every prophecy in the Bible about Israel has been fulfilled. But Jesus is not yet reigning on David's throne over Israel. Therefore, either the angel sent from God was wrong or realised eschatology is wrong.[9]

There are many other prophecies about Israel that have not been fulfilled. Two such will be selected for brief examination and they too make reference to the Davidic covenant.

---

not restricted to his provisional pre-parousia reign, but are addressing, in particular, the post-parousia reign of Christ after his delivery of the kingdom of God. At that point the Christocentric reign is subordinately blended into an eternally established theocentric reign of God and of the Lamb..." (*The Cross and the Parousia of Christ*, page 10). How to make a simple subject difficult!

Another writes, "The perfect covenant came in its completeness in AD 70 which, accordingly, brought with it a whole new 'millennium'. Christ thereafter reigned in a new way in which he had not reigned before the fall of Jerusalem." (M. Hall, *The Cure For Millennial Madness*, page 85.)

8. J. L. Bray, *Bible Prophecy*, page 14.

9. Realised eschatologists recognise the logic of this line of reasoning but get around it by giving the words of the covenant promise their own definition. They argue that David's throne is actually God's throne in heaven and that the house of Jacob over which Jesus is to reign is actually the church. Thus, "He (Jesus) reigns in heaven [now]... We are in the kingdom age." (J. L. Bray, *Bible Prophecy*, page 77).

Jeremiah 30

"For, lo, the days come, saith the LORD, that I will bring again the captivity of my people Israel and Judah, saith the LORD: and I will cause them to return to the land that I gave to their fathers, and they shall possess it... For it shall come to pass in that day, saith the LORD of hosts, that I will break his yoke from off thy neck, and will burst thy bonds, and strangers shall no more serve themselves of him: But they shall serve the LORD their God, and David their king, whom I will raise up unto them." (vv. 3,8,9)

This scripture teaches that all Israel – i.e. Israel and Judah – would be regathered from their captivity and "return to the land that [God] gave to their fathers, and they shall possess it" (v. 3). The realised eschatology position is that this refers solely to the return from the Babylonian captivity.[10] However, this view is ruled out for the prophecy proceeds to speak of the time when the Gentile yoke shall be cast off for ever ("strangers shall **no more** serve themselves of him") and Israel will serve a Davidic king to be raised up for them.

This is in complete harmony with the promise in 2 Samuel 7 and the words of the angel in Luke ch. 1.

This prophecy was not fulfilled at the time of the return from Babylon. It certainly was not fulfilled in the events of AD 70, for Israel has been under Gentile yoke since that time – Roman, Arab and Turk. They have been oppressed and persecuted in the countries of their dispersion. Although there has been a regathering and refounding of the nation in the last 120 years this is not the full restoration envisaged in such restoration prophecies as those being considered. The restoration of Israel (as opposed to the current regathering) involves their repentance and their acceptance of the rulership of Messiah in accordance with the Davidic covenant – a subject that cannot be elaborated in this study.

---

10. E.g. "After they came back into the land of Palestine as a result of the promises of God which said "I will regather my people", there was never another prophecy made about a future gathering in our day..." (J. Bray, *Bible Prophecy*, page 18).

Isaiah 9

"For unto us a child is born, unto us a son is given: and the government shall be upon his shoulder: and his name shall be called Wonderful, Counseller, The mighty God, The everlasting Father, The Prince of Peace. Of the increase of his government and peace there shall be no end, upon the throne of David, and upon his kingdom, to order it, and to establish it with judgment and with justice from henceforth even for ever. The zeal of the LORD of hosts will perform this." (vv. 6,7)

The One who in this prophecy is styled "the Prince of Peace" is to reign on David's throne[11] – a clear reference to the covenant promise of 2 Samuel 7. When he does so reign it is said of him, "Of the increase of his government and peace there shall be **no end**." This is the very phrase used by the angel in Luke ch. 1 – "he shall reign over the house of Jacob for ever; and of his kingdom there shall be **no end**." This has not been fulfilled at any time in Israel's history.

These Old Testament prophecies provide the background against which the teaching of Jesus and the apostles must be viewed. They accepted Old Testament teaching and expected their followers to do the same. The following brief review of some of the teaching of Jesus and his apostles shows that this is so:

1. In Matthew 19:28 Jesus promised the disciples that in the regeneration when the Son of man would sit in the throne of his glory, they would sit on twelve thrones judging the twelve tribes of Israel. The throne of Messiah's glory is the throne of David covenanted to him in 2 Samuel 7 and promised in Luke 1:32, 33. There is nothing in this passage that would lead us to see it as referring to anything other than a restoration of the kingdom of Israel.

2. Clearly, the disciples themselves expected such a restoration for subsequent to the resurrection of Jesus, after he had been with them for 40 days speaking of the things pertaining to the

11. M. King maintains that this was completely fulfilled in AD 70 and sees it as referring to "Christianity an accomplished work of God in Christ that adequately meets the needs of man now and for ever." (*The Cross and the Parousia of Christ*, page 759.)

Kingdom of God, they asked him, "Wilt thou at this time restore again the kingdom to Israel?" Jesus did not say that they were mistaken and the kingdom of Israel would never be restored. He said simply, "It is not for you to know the times or the seasons, which the Father hath put in his own power" (Acts 1:3–7).

3. In Acts ch. 3, Peter, speaking to Jews, refers to the time when God will "send Jesus Christ, which before was preached unto you: Whom the heaven must receive until the time of restitution of all things, which God hath spoken by the mouth of all his holy prophets since the world[12] began" (vv. 20, 21). In no sense can AD 70 be viewed as a restitution or restoration of anything — it was "the end" of the Mosaic system. The restitution of "all things" spoken by the prophets is the restoration of Israel under Messiah their divinely appointed king.

4. The Lord Jesus, in Luke's account of the Olivet Prophecy, indicated his belief in the future restoration of Israel. When speaking of the impending overthrow of Jerusalem by the Romans, he said, "They (the Jews) shall fall by the edge of the sword, and shall be led away captive into all nations: and Jerusalem shall be trodden down of the Gentiles, **until** the times of the Gentiles[13] be fulfilled" (Luke 22:24). The downtreading of the **literal** city of Jerusalem and the scattering and oppression of the Jews was to last for a limited period of time – **until** the times of the Gentiles were expired.

In whatever way realised eschatologists seek to explain these prophecies away, they have to contend with certain stubborn facts that are in harmony with a latter-day fulfilment of the restoration prophecies:

---

12. The Greek word translated "world" here is *kósmos* and refers to the nation of Israel. See footnote 5, page 31.

13. For comments on the meaning of this phrase, "the times of the Gentiles", see pages 49–50.

- The Jews have been preserved in the countries of their dispersion for nigh on two thousand years.
- A regathering of Jews has taken place in the past 120 years — there are now in excess of five million Jews in the land.
- The State of Israel has been re-created.[14]

Since "the most High ruleth in the kingdom of men" (Dan. 4:17) these things cannot be chance happenings.

It must be understood that I am not saying that these events are a complete fulfilment of the restoration prophecies, for that is the work appointed for Messiah on his return. Not until "There shall come out of Sion the Deliverer, and shall turn away ungodliness from Jacob" (Rom. 11:26)[15] will the full restoration spoken of by the prophets be realised.

---

14. King in his treatise on realised eschatology sets out to answer the question— "What about the State of Israel today?" He spends four pages tilting at various eschatological windmills but never gets around to answering the question! (*The Cross and the Parousia of Christ*, pages 745–749). To him the fulfilment of the restoration prophecies have to do with "Christ's world — the world above, or the heavenly country of the Abrahamic promise". He forgets that God said to Abraham, "All ***the land*** which thou seest, to thee will I give it, and to thy seed ***for ever***" (Gen. 13:15), and that it was right there, in "the land of promise" (Heb. 11:9) — ***on this earth*** — that Abraham looked for the "heavenly country".

15. This scripture is speaking of the time when "All Israel shall be saved" (v. 26). These words are often applied by realised eschatologists (and others) to believers. This shows a lack of appreciation of the Old Testament on which the apostle here bases his reasoning. The Old Testament repeatedly refers to the time when ***all Israel*** — i.e. Israel and Judah — will be saved by God. E.g. "For, lo, the days come, saith the LORD, that I will bring again the captivity of my people ***Israel*** and ***Judah***, saith the LORD: and I will cause them to return to the land that I gave to their fathers, and they shall possess it... [and] they shall serve the LORD their God, and ***David their king, whom I will raise up unto them***... For I am with thee, saith the LORD, to ***save thee***..." (Jer. 30:3, 9, 11). "And say unto them, Thus saith the Lord GOD; Behold, I will take the children of Israel from among the heathen, whither they be gone, and will gather them on every side, and bring them into their own land: And I will make them ***one nation*** in the land upon the mountains of Israel; and one king shall be king to them all: and they shall be ***no more two nations,*** neither shall they be divided into two kingdoms any more at all: Neither shall they defile themselves any more with their idols, nor with their detestable things, nor with any of their transgressions: but ***I will save them*** out of all their dwellingplaces, wherein they have sinned, and ***will cleanse***

[Footnote continued on next page]

The Future Appearing of Messiah

God's promises to David, the prophecies of the restoration and the teaching of Jesus and his apostles based on these, demand a future appearing of Jesus Christ. The realised eschatologists argue:

> "The New Testament does not teach two different returns of Christ. He was to return only once, and this happened in the first century when Jerusalem was destroyed! How can he come back again if he hasn't left again? He came in the first century (at AD 70). He hasn't left. He is still present with us. He will always be with us." [16]

This pronouncement by a well known realised eschatologist is full of confusion and conflicting statements and is shown to be untrue by the following:

1. Whilst the New Testament clearly teaches the coming (in AD 70) of Christ in judgement against Israel, we have shown that the Bible also teaches a restoration of Israel's kingdom. There is to be a restitution of the house of Jacob over which Jesus is to reign for ever. This demands a future appearing of Jesus. It is of this appearing that the apostle speaks when he says, "The Lord Jesus Christ… shall judge the quick and the dead at **his appearing** *and* **his kingdom**" (2 Tim. 4:1).

2. The statement from E. E. Stevens quoted above argues that Jesus came in AD 70 and never left but has been with his followers **ever since** — in fact he is always with us. To say that Jesus has been with his followers since AD 70 appears to

---

them: so shall they be my people, and I will be their God. And ***David my servant shall be king*** over them; and they all shall have one shepherd: they shall also walk in my judgments, and observe my statutes, and do them. And they shall dwell in the land that I have given unto Jacob my servant, wherein your fathers have dwelt; and they shall dwell therein, even they, and their children, and their children's children for ever: and my servant David shall be their prince for ever" (Ezek. 37:21–25). Thus the time when "all Israel shall be saved" is the time when Messiah, the Son of David (Matt. 1:1) comes to take up his covenanted position as king on David's throne. It will be at that time that he will "turn away ungodliness from Jacob".

16. E. E. Stevens, *What Happened in AD 70?*, page 6.

contradict the teaching of Jesus when he said to his disciples, "Lo, I am with you alway, even **unto** the end of the world" (Matt. 28:20). The "end of the world" (rendered in the RSV "the close of the age") is the same "end of the world" as in Matthew 24:3, i.e. the end of the nation of Israel organised under the Law covenant. This teaches that Jesus would be with the disciples from the time of his ascension **until** AD 70. It should also be noted that Jesus said **to his disciples**, "Where two or three are gathered together in my name, there am I in the midst of them" (Matt. 18:20). He was not talking of something that would come into effect after AD 70. He was talking of the situation that would prevail in the apostolic church — i.e. before, and leading up to, AD 70.

Thus, it is evident that for Jesus to be with his followers is nothing to do with the AD 70 coming in judgement against Israel. He was with them before AD 70. In what way Jesus was with the disciples then, is beyond the scope of this study. This nearness of Jesus to his followers is quite different from his coming in judgement against Israel in AD 70, and quite different from his future coming to "sit upon the throne of his glory" (Matt. 25:31).

Resurrection

The appearing of Jesus to restore David's kingdom is associated by Paul with the judging of the living and the dead (2 Tim. 4:1). The resurrection of the "dead in Christ" at his future coming is a clear teaching of scripture. In 1 Corinthians 15 there are some very plain statements, which defy all attempts to argue away the doctrine of a future resurrection. The letter was written, in part, to put right some who taught, "there is no resurrection of the dead" (vv. 12, 13). The following teaching of Paul should be conclusive for those who are willing to accept the authority of scripture.

1. Jesus Christ was raised from the dead (vv. 1-20). The realised eschatologists accept that this was a bodily resurrection.[17]
2. The apostle states that "In Adam all die" – as previously shown death is the natural lot of all Adam's children. Paul proceeds to say that "In Christ shall all be made alive" – those who are "in Christ" (i.e. Christ's children by being born again, 1 Pet. 1:23; 1 John 3:2), will be made alive.
3. This "making alive" of those in Christ will be at a time referred to as "the last trump" (1 Cor. 15:52). Elsewhere, this same apostle associates this with the appearing of the Lord – "The Lord himself shall descend from heaven with a shout, with the voice of the archangel, and with the trump of God: and the dead in Christ shall rise first" (1 Thess. 4:16).
4. The resurrection will be a bodily resurrection, for the giving of immortality is by change from mortal to immortal – "this mortal must put on immortality" (1 Cor. 15:53).[18] Elsewhere the apostle teaches that Jesus "shall change our vile body, that it may be fashioned like unto his glorious body" (Phil. 3:21). The resurrection of Jesus was bodily. The resurrection of the dead in Christ will also be bodily.[19]

---

17. "The New Testament bears witness to the real and tangible quality of Jesus' resurrection body." (R. C. Leonard & J. E. Leonard, *The Promise of His Coming*, page 162.)

18. Note: this is the reverse of the immortal soul teaching, which in effect says that the immortal shall cast off the mortal.

19. It is amazing that one of the chief protagonists of realised eschatology spends 220 pages in a book of some 700 pages in an attempt to show that 1 Corinthians 15 does not refer to bodily resurrection! He sets out what he calls an "alternate view" and argues, if I have understood his reasoning correctly, that Paul was not speaking of bodily resurrection but of the death of Israel under the Law covenant and of the emergence of Christianity, the new Israel. He goes through the entire chapter of 1 Corinthians 15 setting out very complicated arguments with the intention of showing that none of the verses in the chapter mean what they appear to be saying. (M. King, *The Cross and the Parousia of Christ*, pages 429–648.)

THE LORD'S MOUNT OLIVET PROPHECY

Those faithful followers of Jesus whose bodies will be resurrected and changed will enjoy their immortality on the earth. They will share with Jesus in the great work of filling this earth with God's glory. This was the teaching of the apostle Paul when he wrote, "If we suffer [with him], we shall also reign with him" (2 Tim. 2:12). From Jerusalem, the centre of Messiah's kingdom, there will emanate a powerful and irresistible movement for peace; a peace based on right living before God.

> "And it shall come to pass in the last days, that the mountain of the LORD's house shall be established in the top of the mountains, and shall be exalted above the hills; and all nations shall flow unto it. And many people shall go and say, Come ye, and let us go up to the mountain of the LORD, to the house of the God of Jacob; and he will teach us of his ways, and we will walk in his paths: for out of Zion shall go forth the law, and the word of the LORD from Jerusalem. And he shall judge among the nations, and shall rebuke many people: and they shall beat their swords into plowshares, and their spears into pruninghooks: nation shall not lift up sword against nation, neither shall they learn war any more." (Isa. 2:2–4)

> "For unto us a child is born, unto us a son is given: and the government shall be upon his shoulder: and his name shall be called Wonderful, Counseller, The mighty God, The everlasting Father, The Prince of Peace. Of the increase of his government and peace there shall be no end, upon the throne of David, and upon his kingdom, to order it, and to establish it with judgment and with justice from henceforth even for ever. The zeal of the LORD of hosts will perform this." (Isa. 9:6–7)

Conclusion

Belief in the fulfilment of the Olivet Prophecy in AD 70 is not the sole preserve of realised eschatology. This scripturally sustainable exposition was set out by a number of esteemed Bible students long before the appearance of the system of teaching called realised eschatology. Such an understanding of the Olivet Prophecy does not in any way interfere with a belief in the future appearing of Messiah. The scriptures clearly teach that Christ is yet to appear:

1. To raise the dead in Christ to life eternal.
2. To restore the nation of Israel and bring these people to repentance.

3. To reign on David's throne in Jerusalem and from thence to make his foes his footstool introducing an unprecedented era of righteousness and peace in the earth.

BIBLIOGRAPHY

Abbott-Smith, G. *Manual Greek Lexicon of the New Testament*
T&T Clark, Edinburgh, UK, 1937.

Agar-Beet, J. *The Immortality of the Soul*
Hodder & Stoughton, London, UK, 1901.

Alford, H. *New Testament For English Readers*
Rivingtons, Cambridge, UK, 1872.

Allfree, J. *A World Destroyed By Fire*
Bible Study Publications, Mansfield, UK, 1994.

—— *Expository Notes On Ephesians*
Bible Study Publications, Mansfield, UK, 1996.

—— *Trinitarian Texts Examined*
Bible Study Publications, Mansfield, UK, 2005.

Archbishops of Canterbury & York *Towards the Conversion of England*
Church Assembly, London, UK, 1945.

Beasley-Murray, G. R. *Jesus and the Future*
Macmillan & Co. Ltd., London, UK, 1954.

Beale, M. *Concerning a Third Jewish Temple*
Testimony, Volume 75, Norwich, UK, 2005.

Ben-Sasson, H. H. *A History of the Jewish People*
Harvard University Press, Cambridge, Mass., USA, 1976.

Benson, T. *Interpreting the Mount Olivet Prophecy*
Testimony, vol. 65, Norwich, UK, 1995.

—— *Olivet Prophecy* (Editorial Comment)
Testimony, vol. 66, Norwich, UK, 1996.

Brandon, S. G. F. *The Fall of Jerusalem and the Christian Church*
SPCK, London, UK, 1951.

Bray, J. L. *Matthew 24 Fulfilled*
PO Box 90129, Lakeland, Florida, USA, 1996.

—— *Bible Prophecy*
PO Box 90129, Lakeland, Florida, USA, 1993

Brown, C. *The Truth About the Olivet Prophecy*
The Way Ahead: March/April, Orpington, UK, 2003..

Bruce, F. F. *Israel and the Nations*
Paternoster Press, Exeter, UK, 1963.

—— *The Book of Acts*
Marshall, Morgan & Scott, Ltd., London, UK, 1954.

Clarke, A. *Bible Commentary* (Electronic Version)
PC Study Bible, Biblesoft Inc., Seattle, WA, USA, 2003.

DeHaan, M. R. *The Jew and Palestine in Prophecy*
Zondervan, Grand Rapids, USA, 1950.

Deissmann, G. A. *Light From the Ancient East* (27th Edition Reprint)
Hendrickson, Peabody, Mass., USA, 1995.

Eusebius *Ecclesiastical History* (C. F. Cruse edition)
George Bell & Sons, London, UK, 1879.

Faulkner, N. *Apocalypse: The Great Jewish Revolt Against Rome AD 66-73*
Tempus Publishing, Stroud, UK, 2002.

Fowler, H. *The Gospel of Matthew*
College Press, Joplin, USA, 1968.

Friedrich, G. and Kittel, G. — *Theological Dictionary of the New Testament*
Eerdmans, Grand Rapids, USA, 1964–1976.

Gesenius — *Hebrew and Chaldee Lexicon*
Eerdmans, Grand Rapids, USA, 1949.

Godet, F. — *The Gospel of St. Luke*
T&T Clark, Edinburgh, UK, 1870.

Grayzel, S. — *A History of the Jews*
Penguin, Markham, Ontario, Canada, 1968.

Gribetz, J. et al. — *The Timetables of Jewish History*
Simon & Schuster, New York, USA, 1993.

Hall, M. — *The Cure For Millennial Madness*
Empowerment Technologies, Grand Jctn, USA, 1994.

Hastings, J. — *Dictionary of Christ and the Gospels*
T&T Clark, Edinburgh, UK, 1906.

Haward, A. — *Great News for the World*
Christadelphians Worldwide: Birmingham, UK, 1976.

Heaster, D. — *The Last Days*
Pioneer Publications, London, UK, 1992.

—— — *Beyond Bible Basics*
Christadelphian Advancement Trust, Croydon, UK, 1999.

Hicks, O. — *The AD 70 Theory*
Gospel Enterprises, Searcy, USA, ND.

Humphreys, E. — *The Mount Olivet Prophecy*
Testimony vol. 47, Hereford, UK, 1977.

Josephus, F. — *The Works of Flavius Josephus* (Whiston's Edition)
Wm. Nimmo, Edinburgh, UK, 1865.

King, M. — *The Cross and the Parousia of Christ*
Parkman Rd. Church of Christ, Warren, USA, 1949.

Kik, J. M. — *An Eschatology of Victory*
Presbyterian & Reformed, Phillipsburg, USA, 1971.

Knowles, J. — *The Olivet Prophecy*
Menorah Publications, St. Agnes, S. Australia, ND.

Leonard, R.C. & J.E. — *The Promise of His Coming*
Laudemont Press, Chicago, USA, 1996.

Lightfoot, J. — *Commentary on the New Testament from the Talmud and Hebraica,*
Hendrickson, USA, 1995.

Lindsey, H. — *The Late Great Planet Earth*
Lakeland, London, 1970.

McClintock, J. & Strong, J. — *Cyclopaedia of Biblical, Theological and Ecclesiastical Literature*
Baker, USA, 1968.

Mansfield, H. P. — *Guidebook to the Gospels*
Logos, West Beach, S. Australia, ND.

Marshall, J. — *The Olivet Prophecy*
CIL Bible Study Notes, Birmingham, UK, 1972.

Milman, H.H. — *The History of the Jews*
Routledge, London, UK, circa 1894.

Newton, T. — *Dissertations on the Prophecies*
Henry Washbourne, London, UK, circa 1804.

Olshausen, H. — *Commentary on the Gospels*
T&T Clark, Edinburgh, UK, 1847.

Osborne, P. L. — *Rome Versus Jerusalem*
Testimony, vols. 74 & 75, Norwich, UK, 2004–05

Roberts, R. — *The Ways of Providence*
CMPA, Birmingham, UK, 1912.

—— — *Three Alleged Failures in the Prophecies of Christ* (Answer to)
The Christadelphian, vol. 35, Birmingham, UK, 1898.

—— — *Was Redemption Nigh in the Apostolic Age?* (Answer to)
The Christadelphian, vol. 14, Birmingham, UK, 1877.

Robinson, J. A. T. — *Redating the New Testament*
SCM Press Ltd., London, UK, 1977.

Rotherham, J. B. — *The Emphasised Bible*
Kregel, Grand Rapids, USA, 1959.

Russell, C.. T. — *Studies in the Scriptures,* (Reprint)
Dawn Bible Students Assoc., East Rutherford, USA, 1961.

Russell, J. S. — *The Parousia*
Daldy, Isbister & Co., London, UK, 1878.

Sargent, H. N. — *The Marvels of Bible Prophecy*
Covenant Publishing Co. Ltd., London, 1940.

Schor, S. — *The Everlasting Nation and Their Coming King*
Prophetic Witness, Eastbourne, UK, 1933.

Stevens, E. E. — *What Happened in AD 70?*
The Author, Bradford, PA, USA, 1988.

Stevenson, J. — *A New Eusebius*
SPCK, London, UK, 1959.

Southgate, P.J. — *Light on Israel [Light Magazine, vol. 6.1]*
Dawn Book Supply, London, UK, ND.

Tacitus — *The Histories* (Trans. K. Wellesley)
Penguin Books, Harmondsworth, UK, 1964.

Thayer, J. H. — *Greek English Lexicon of the New Testament*
Hendrickson Publishers inc., Peabody, Mass., USA, 1996.

Thomas, J. — *Eureka — An Exposition of the Apocalypse*
Dawn Book Supply, London, UK, 1959.

—— — *The Prophecy of Mount Olivet*
Herald of the Kingdom and Age to Come, vol. 3, NY, USA, 1853.

—— — *Promises Covenanted to David*
Herald of the Kingdom and Age to Come, vol. 8, NY, USA, 1858.

—— — *The Last Days of Judah's Commonwealth*
Herald of the Kingdom and Age to Come, vol. 9, NY, USA, 1859.

—— — *The Prophecy of Mount Olivet*
Herald of the Kingdom and Age to Come, vol. 10, NY, USA, 1860.

Vine, W. E. — *Expository Dictionary of New Testament Words*
Oliphants, London, UK, 1940.

Waddington, G. — *A History of the Church*
Baldwin & Craddock, London, UK, 1833.

Waite, G. — *Watchman, What of the Night?*
The Christadelphian, vol. 62, Birmingham, UK, 1925.

Walker, C. C. *This Generation* (Answer to correspondent)
The Christadelphian, vol. 54, Birmingham, UK, 1917.

Whittaker, E. *The Mount Olivet Prophecy*
Testimony, vol. 51, Norwich, UK, 1981.

Whittaker, H.A. *Studies in the Gospels*
Biblia, Cannock, UK, ND.

Wilson, B. *The Emphatic Diaglott*
International Bible Students Assoc., Brooklyn, USA, 1942.

Wright, N. T. *The New Testament and the People of God*
SPCK, London, 1992.

Young, R. *Literal Translation of the Bible*
Fullerton, London, UK, 1863.

Zodhiates, S. *The Complete Word Study Dictionary: New Ttestament*
AMG, Chattanooga, USA, 1992.